My Heroes, My Town

Conversations With A Child

Nikos Ligidakis

INKWELL BOOKS

Writing - Publishing - Printing

For My Parents

ISBN: 978-1-939625-8-61
Library of Congress Control Number: 2018912344

Published by Inkwell Books LLC
10632 North Scottsdale Road, Unit 695
Scottsdale, AZ 85254
Tel. 480-315-3781
E-mail info@inkwellbooksllc.com
Website www.inkwellbooksllc.com

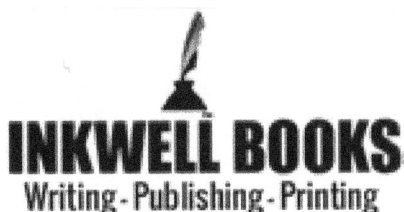

INKWELL BOOKS
Writing - Publishing - Printing

This book demonstrates how the lessons learned from our childhood experiences evolve into knowledge and wisdom on each consecutive stride of our life's trials.

Table of Contents

1

THE TAVERNA

As a child, I had the desire to understand all things. It was my curiosity that led me to level my ears into conversations of the elders who had gathered in my father's taverna. Time and again, words of wisdom were spoken by the crowd who frequented the taverna. They told stories about brave people, sang songs about life and love, and seemed content with the simplicity of their lifestyle.

The taverna seemed to be everyone's happy place. It was a small narrow room overflowing with vital energy. Provocative scents of foods were dispersing from its open kitchen, while the wine pouring from the oak barrel's wooden spigot sprinkled a tantalizing aroma across the room. The savory element and the boisterous energy from the patrons remain a deafening image that will follow me until the end of time.

Amidst the laughter, songs and folktales about heroic deeds and mythical characters, there was my father's smile and my mother's luminous face.

The faces and voices of the fishermen, the farmers, the laborers and all who frequented the taverna, have remained towering figures in my imagination. The wit and wisdom of their tales seemed to capture the meaning of moral principles. It was the taverna crowd that led me on to an unending path of exploration about heroic deeds and the importance of character. Since my youth, I have walked on a narrow path between the new and the old. The future was fascinating, the new advances due to human brilliance were riveting, and yet, the charming era of the Bohemian lifestyle of the past, was entrapped in my psyche.

The eternal question of how to measure my worth has always been a tormenting component in my child's mind. Was I to gain social prestige and substantial wealth to feel important, or to be content with simplicity and pursue harmony? Which one of the two theoretical worlds must I adopt for my primary existence and which one should let slip through the cracks of tediousness?

My parents wanted me to go to school, to get educated, to live a better life. I honored their wish. However, my most valuable teachings have always been from those whom I admired, and the lessons learned from life's realities. One of my earliest and most valuable lessons was while serving my mandatory duty in the military. That period was my bridge from childhood to adulthood. There was much there that I loved; country, patriotism, solidarity, and much I despised; guns, tyranny and pettiness. There were lessons of responsibility, friendship but most importantly, it unleashed the awareness of an independent lifestyle; away from mother's care and father's protectiveness.

I struggled with the question of how to achieve the simplicity of the past while living in a boisterous and glamorous society. The answer remained hidden within me for a long time. During those times, harmony seemed to be a moving target; a lifelong pursuit of unreachable perfection.

Along the way many things seemed to unbalance the natural

order; human rights violations, elder abuse, mistreatment of children, destroying the earth, poverty, and corrupt power. It was an impassable burden of trying to understand the virtues and the ineptness of those who changed the social landscape and for those who stigmatized it.

During my life's struggles, I often closed my eyes to escape the troubling moments and took an imaginary journey to my happy place; the taverna. From there, I strolled through the small streets of my beloved town or imagined laying under the sun as the sea waves were touching my feet; and once again the world seemed a peaceful place.

Among the elders who impressed me with their words and deeds, two people became my biggest heroes. The two individuals who were and will always walk along with me in my life. Two traditional people who taught me about kindness and perseverance.

They gave me life, love, and smiles, but I paid them back with worries about my ongoing adventures.

As they infused me with wisdom and compassion, I gave them many headaches while searching for advanced theories. When they paved a single road for me to walk on, I choose to be lost on the world's multi-line highways.

My parents did not try to save the world; their effort was limited to impact the small circle around them; first their family and then the community they lived in. It was because of their approach that my perspective about harmony and character was framed into limiting myself to positive surroundings.

The taverna was where my parents worked.

My mother was the ruler of our home. My father was the dominant figure in the taverna.

My mother was also the adopted mother of all our friends. Our friends loved to come to our home, to be spoiled by mother's sweets and to talk to her. She could reach out and advise them about their young life's concerns. Often, they would say to me, "Your mom is witty and so wise." I would shrivel up my shoulders and say, "really?" I didn't see what they saw in her; she was my Mom whose heart was an ocean of love.

My father's powerful energy and my mother's tender strength created an astounding balance in my young life. My parents had denied themselves every convenience and luxury of their lives to devote all of their energy to their five children.

As I am writing, my mind goes back to the last summer I spent in Kiato with my dad. It was the end of the summer of sixty-nine. We drove to Kiato with a group of our friends, ten or twelve I believe, to celebrate my release from the military. My father was delighted to see us. Anytime we visited Kiato with friends, no matter how many, my dad always opened his welcoming arms. We all gathered in the taverna and dad cooked for us. He made sure that we had everything we needed to have a good time. All my friends loved my father, and they often talked about his strength, wisdom, and kindness. To me, he was just my father, the one that I've always respected. However, that summer, after my friends pointed out his compassion and wisdom, I noticed something special that towered in front of me. There was a model of a man, one that never gave up despite the many challenges. The few weeks that I spent with him in the summer of sixty-nine was the most memorable times of my life. It was as if I wanted to absorb every fiber of my father's persona. All my life's emotions have concealed in that time-frame and perched at the edge of my consciousness; a feeling that remains a blissful sentiment. It is an emotion that emerges in my dark moments to remind me of the magnificence of the human soul. That was the last summer I spent with my father. The last time I saw him alive.

My Heroes, My Town

2

MY TOWN

Kiato is where I first saw the lights of this world; it is where my mother nourished, and my father disciplined me.

The town of Kiato is nestled in the Corinthian Gulf at the northeast part of the Peloponnese Peninsula. Peloponnese is linked to the mainland by a bridge that hangs over the Isthmus of Corinth. The canal was opened in 1893 to shorten the passage from east to west by way of the sea. It is about five miles long. Peloponnese is unique because of its scenic beauty and endless archaeological sites, where the past is so vividly present.

As you pass the isthmus, driving east, you will find a plethora of souvenir shops and restaurants. A few minutes further is the town of Corinth, and a few kilometers north is the ancient city of Corinth. Driving on the old highway by the sea, you will pass several villages before you get to Kiato. The scenery is breathtaking. Endless vineyards, citrus trees, and olive tree fields are soaring above the blue sea.

Kiato was one of those small towns where life passes slowly. In the evening thousands of people stepped out of their homes to socialize.

On the agora's main street, there was the Kostakias Cafe

where people would sit outside and have a snack or drink of beer. Across the street from it was my uncle's jewelry store. As children, we would run inside to see our uncles. They always greeted us with smiles and gave us a few drachmas so we could buy treats.

Down the main street past the endless storefronts was a large coffee shop. It was always full of people, some playing backgammon or cards, others argued about politics and football. Further down the street was the bus station from which buses left for various towns and villages. Across the street from the bus station was the taxi cab line, if you needed a cab driver you had to search in the coffee shop to find him.

Shortly after the sun vanishes in the far horizon, the town's people jammed the main street. Old and young, wealthy and poor walked together.

Clothing stores, shoe shops, general stores, and shops of all kinds displayed their merchandise in their storefront. Everything was available on that main street. Further down the main street, there was the Tsalikis pastry shop with its display cases full of luscious cakes and pastries. Across the street there was the Paparas restaurant with a full menu and tables with white tablecloths.

As you walked down the festive main street, it was like an exciting adventure. When the evening was coming to a close and most of the people had gone home, it felt like the ending of a classic movie. But then the next day would become like a dream world again. It was an excitement that has become a paradigm of joyfulness. The agora was the combination of many things. On the main street, all people were influential and respected; women, children, teenagers, married couples, elders, the priest, the mayor, they were all present.

The street was as if every child's dream had become a reality. The pastry shops with their luscious desserts, ice cream shops, roasted nuts, fried loukoumades dipped in honey and cinnamon; it was a feast to satisfy a child's mind.

That main street was the town's cultural center. Our teachers walked that street, and we would hide to avoid questions about our homework. The Priest walked there often, dressed in his traditional black robe and everyone bowed their heads respectfully as he went by.It was on that street that I learned so much about life. Everyone had a job to do during the day, but after sunset, everyone had a place in the spotlight. Further down the street was the Karamalikis Ouzeri and across from that the charming Androutsos bookstore. Next to it was the small hotel with its marble floors and stairways. The hotel guests sat on the iron-fenced balcony looking down the street. At the end of the road, there were more coffee shops where hundreds of people sat outside facing the town's square. Above the coffee shops was the Mayor's office with the Greek flag hanging from its balcony.

On one corner of the town square, there was a water fountain running cold water from the deep earth. At the other corner of the square was the kiosk with candies, newspapers, and magazines widely displayed. The only paper not to be found was a local newspaper. There was no need for one. All the local news was broadcasted by the people on the main street every evening.

Across from the kiosk was the Holevas yogurt shop where homemade yogurt and honey was served on marble-top tables. As you walked down that narrow street on your way to the sea, there were tables tucked between the vines and the palm trees. They were always full of people having ice cream from the Pitines shops.

A short wrought-iron fence surrounded by trees and plants enclosed the square. Inside the square was lovely landscaping with flowers and wood benches for people to rest. In the middle of the square, a statue of freedom fighters and a water fountain sprinkling water to the surrounding plants.

In that square, life was visible as you saw children playing with joy, teenage boys getting the courage to talk to the young girls, and elders sitting on the benches relaxing.

Past the square was a street that ran along the beach-front and beyond that street was the town's small port, built from giant cement blocks. A few fishing boats were docked to the side. During the day many people were fishing, and hundreds of swimmers would dive into the clear blue water.

Walking by the beach, beyond the soccer field, couples sat by the seawater creating dreams under the moonlight. Further down was the church of Agia Sotira. You couldn't miss it because it occupied the entire square block. Restoration of the church began when I was a little boy, and it resulted in a modern architectural wonder. West of the church, across the street, was our school. The two-story building boasted windows all around, most of them overlooking the sea.

Directly across the street from the church, you pass the small high school and Klis bicycle shop, Gizariotis shoe repair shop and next to it Smimoglou General Store. It was full of candy and was the children's popular destination. Next to it was my father's taverna. Next to the taverna in the corner was Flokas butcher shop and around the corner was Karagounis fishery.

My father's long and narrow taverna contained four tables on each side pushed up against the wall. There was a total of thirty-four seats. A long table separated the kitchen from the eating area. The cooking area was small. A custom-made block of cement with three-square L-shaped openings. The bottom opening was where the wood burned and the top opening was used to cook the food. Everything was cooked on a wood fire. The top of the counter was laid with tile and kept the foods warm. Baked items were prepared in the taverna and taken to a nearby bakery to be baked in their wood burning oven. Bread was bought fresh daily from the bakery. Next to the stove, in the corner, was a small washing area. A large basin filled with water from the fountain across the street was used for washing the dishes. Next, to the sink, there was a small wooden refrigerator. The box was kept cold by blocks of ice and it stored, mainly, cold beers. Next to it were the wine oak barrels.

The entire setting was simple and practical. There were no menus; a blackboard by the kitchen described the three or four specials of the day. Outside, on the sidewalk to the right of the door stood an iron barbecue stand where all the roasted specialties were prepared. On the other side of the door were three more tables and across the busy road, there were more dining tables tucked between the vines.

My parents worked hard to operate the taverna, my father cooked and they both served and washed dishes.

The house where we lived was about a ten-minute walk to the west, along the beach. The house had wooden floors, a long hallway down the middle of it which connected the front and back doors. Two rooms were on each side of the entrance. On one side were my parent's bedroom and the living room. On the other side was the kitchen with a table to eat, a fireplace and the children's bedroom. Outside, in the backyard, my mother kept her animals and her garden. Deeper in the yard was a small barn which housed the chickens and a few hand-made cabinets with wire doors to keep rabbits. The goat and the pig ran loose in the yard. Trees consisted of fig, lemon, orange, and pomegranate and were joined by the vegetable and herb gardens. And, of course, flowers. My mother loved flowers and birds. Flowers planted in pots grew all over the yard. Several cages of colorful singing birds hung outside.

My mom showered us out in the backyard, she dumped a bucket of water over our heads, scrubbed us with her homemade soap. Sometimes we screamed and pretended that our eyes were burning from the soap. "How can you torture your children like that?" we complained, you know, as kids do because let's face it kids don't like showers. Then she dumped another bucket of water over our head to wash out the soap and on we went, barefooted and happy.

Our four-legged protector, Jack, a black German Shepherd, was always happy to see us in the backyard. Sometimes he waited at the end of the yard to go swimming with us in our pool. The beautiful blue sea of the Corinthian Gulf was just a few steps beyond the backyard. That was our swimming pool.

In the mid-morning, along with some of my siblings, we would dive in and stay for hours until we got hungry. Then we would run into the taverna to eat and return home for our mandatory afternoon nap, a time when life on the streets stopped. In the evenings, we walked in the agora's busy streets.

When the people left the agora, to go back home, we were hungry. We ran into the taverna, where my father was glad to dish out his masterpieces to any of his children. He smiled while watching us consume the food with great satisfaction. Both father and mother would always encourage us to eat; you see times were difficult in those years. After Hitler and his gangsters had ravaged our country, food and jobs were scarce. My parents went hungry during the years of the German occupation and now they did not want their children to go through such horrific times. "Eat, eat," they would always say.

After the taverna closes for the night, my dad would join his friends to eat, drink, sing and laugh.

My Heroes, My Town

3

SURVIVAL

This one feeling is frozen in time. It is rooted deep in my psyche, behind thick walls of intense emotions and superficial desires. It is an impulse submerged deep into a cosmos of mystery, an instinct that has closed its barriers to the conventional wisdom and logic.

Since I was a child, I have always identified with this mysterious warrior who is quietly hidden in my subconscious mind. Only occasionally this lonely warrior rises to fight a profound battle against alarming forces. The first time this warrior was awakened was a long time ago when my young body was wrapped in the thickness of the salty waters of the Corinthian Sea. I remember feeling trapped inside the crystalline shape of the sea. There was the mystical darkness that surrounded me, and I felt as if an iron net was wrapped around my heart. My air, the symbol of my freedom, was taken away and I was certain that my existence was about to expire.

As I fell into the abyss, this mystic warrior ascended to my defense.

A powerful wave penetrated my body. The chain that bound my heart broke and as I was sinking into the deep waters, a voice shouted at me.

"You must survive…you must!" The voice, unconvincing at first, did not help me resist the fall and further down to the deep I went.

As I sank deeper into the sea, the water pressure intensified. I felt that at any moment a great explosion would erupt and rip my body into multiple pieces of flesh and bones. I was desperate for someone's help. But there was no one to stop me from sinking into the abyss, into confusion.

Suddenly a loud voice from inside of me confronted the powerful sensation of fear that had paralyzed my senses. At that time, I felt two enormous powers clashing inside my chest. One of those powerful creatures was trying to persuade me to give up, to stay entrapped. The other encouraged me to resist, to break free.

It was an unfamiliar emotion as if I had no control over my fate as if I belonged to no realm of reality. That moment it was my introduction to two Titans. I named one of them Fear and the other Courage.

The first one had paralyzed my senses as it was trying to drag me deeper down.

The second one heartened my spirits trying to convince me to endure the danger.

My young life was surrounded by people whose courage spread to the heavens. I was determined not to let them see me cry from fear. I would not allow anyone to notice panic on my face. The clash of the two Titans became a ferocious battle. "I am not afraid…I am brave…," I repeated over and over. Under the waters of my beloved sea, at each moment the voice of the Titan named Courage grew louder.

I pressed my lips together tightly, I furrowed my brow, and I gritted my teeth, my fists opened, the palms of my hands pushed the water down and I began to ascend slowly.

The powerful hands of Fear grasped my legs, holding me down.

But Courage had already embraced my body, lifting me up from the watery grave.

"Be strong…kick your feet…you can do it," he whispered in my ear.

I did just that. Suddenly my body lifted, on the way to survival, straight up like a powerful arrow I went. My head broke the surface of the water, splattering the air with thousands of crystalline drops, and out from my watery grave I went, victorious and brave.

I gasped for air, two, three deep breaths, my lungs yearned for oxygen.

Down I went again, a swallow of salty water plunged into my stomach, back into the darkness I was wrapped once again. The water tasted strange, unlike any other taste I knew. It was bitter, mysterious, intriguing, like the taste of danger.

"I am not afraid…I am not…not me."

My arms opened like two giant wings, they flapped with force, my feet kicked the enormous body of water as the urgency for survival overcame my heart.

The confidence of victory was planted in my mind, and up I went again, out from the deep. Two long breaths and down I let myself sink. This time I did not swallow the salty water. The darkness beneath the water had disappeared now.

A blue light was turned on from the bottom of the sea, a view that allowed me to see the beauty of the rocks, the plants, the sea life. There was a magical world hidden down there.

Now I had identified the enemy; the Titan called Fear. I looked him right in the eyes and mocked him. True, he towered in front of me, but I no longer feared him. I was shielded behind another giant, the one called Courage.

My love affair with the sea began that day. Bonding with the courageous Titan became an integral part of my existence. The fascination with the beautiful and the mysterious was infused into my veins for eternity. I understood that it was possible to communicate with the beast living inside of me, that it was possible to be his friend.

My body pierced the water surface with force. There was a triumphant feeling in my heart, a smile on my face.

"I won…I won…I survived!"

And down I went, again and again. Now I knew how to escape the monster, how to survive. Now the vast waters of the sea were mine, and I was theirs.

Up and down I went, surfacing like a little dolphin, exhaling like a small whale.

The four people around me began to celebrate, rubbing my hair with love, patting me on the back, throwing me up in the air. It was a hero's welcome. My chest puffed up with pride.

One of my uncles smiled at me with love. He was sitting on the boat watching me. My other uncle and two of their friends were swimming in the waters around me, to help me, if needed.

I was five years old that fateful day, that day when courage began to rise in my heart, and immeasurably changed my life forever. Before long I was stroking on top of the great waters and out further from the beach I went. Before long, I sank myself into the bosom of the sea. A superior force, hidden within me, erupted as survival became an essential desire; it sprang forth the virtue of courage.

As I grew older and swam deeper into the sea and as I ran further on the streets, I knew that I was searching for one of the Titans: the one named Fear. I wanted to confront him once more, to look him in the eyes again.

My search went on for years, but I could not find him.

Was it possible that he was dead?

My Heroes, My Town

4

WISDOM AND TEARS

The Second World War devastated Europe's economy. In Greece, more than one million people were left homeless, a quarter of the country's buildings demolished, over one thousand villages destroyed, and more than half of all transportation equipment was damaged.

The material damage from the war amounted to more than four billion dollars.

These numbers do not measure the social and moral impact on the Greek people.

Traditional values, the wealth of social relationships and trust we all rely on to build a thriving social structure were damaged, making it much harder to recover from the overall devastation.

Thousands of families struggled for survival and many businesses shut their doors, some permanently, others temporary. My grandfather's taverna was among those places.

Shortly after the war ended, my father decided to reopen the taverna. Since there were no jobs available and three young children to feed, and more to come, my father thought the taverna was an opportunity to provide for the family. At first, it was difficult, not only because of the poverty-stricken population but he didn't know much about cooking.

My grandfather, weakened by illness and weary of old age, taught my dad the basics of cooking and about wine qualities. Slowly the economy showed signs of recovery; new jobs were created, and tourists began to arrive. The beautiful Corinthian coast is a short drive away from many larger cities and it was affordable for many families to holiday there. My grandfather passed away the same year after reopening of the taverna, leaving only my grandmother and my mother to help father with cooking.

Before long, the locals made the taverna their favorite spot.

For years to come, the reputation of my father's cooking resulted in people coming from as far as Athens to taste his food. The taverna became a favorite spot for travelers as well, who made it a point to stop in Kiato to have a meal and enjoy the wine.

Wine, a predominant part of the Greek life, also drew frequent visits of local customers.

My father knew how to pick the best wines. When it was time to fill the wooden barrels with wine, he sampled several of wines brought to him by wine-makers from nearby villages. A hot Mediterranean climate is the defining feature of the Provence of Corinthia. It is where low-acid oranges grow succulent and aromatic. So, it's no accident that most of the grapes planted in the region are dominant and unabashedly Greek. When you leave Kiato for the northern mountainous villages you drive by orchards of citrus trees, yellow and purple wildflowers and the imposing rock slopes. Endless vineyards are climbing by the mountain roads. The culture of growing grapes and making wine in this astonishing region of the Peloponnese Peninsula has a rich history that dates to ancient times. It is where my father traveled to fill his five oak barrels with his chosen wine.

I remember as a child seeing him leave with the empty barrels loaded on one of those motorcycles with a sidecar. With my father riding on the back of the bike, the driver took him away in the morning and brought him back in the evening with the barrels full of the precious cargo. I remember watching every time they left, wondering about villages, country roads and green lands. In my child's mind, he was going to a distant world, to places I wanted to explore someday.

When father returned in the evening, all of us children were glad to see him even though the time for us to misbehave was over. My mother always threatened that if we didn't listen to her, we would be punished when dad returned. Of course, when he returned, safe and happy to see us, all was forgotten and forgiven.

As the years went by and the children grew up, my parents began thinking about our future and what would be the best way for us to be prepared for a better life. My two older brothers, Lefteris and Andreas, showed interest in the jewelry business. My uncles provided work for them in their jewelry stores and trained them to repair watches and learn the art of jewelry making. Only Lefteris continued to perfect the craft that he made his lifetime profession. Andreas went to the Naval Academy.

I didn't like working in the jewelry stores. In fact, rarely was I willing to help in the taverna. I wanted to be out on the field kicking the soccer ball – that was my universe.

My youngest brother, Giorgos, was the only one who went daily to the taverna to help. He was always there helping, wearing his little white apron. There was an amazing kindness in that little boy and everyone loved him. I loved him too because he would share his earnings with me from time to time.

My sister, Sofia, was the best student of the family, always good in school. She took her education further than the rest of us. Although all the siblings shared a resemblance in looks, my resemblance with Sofia was much more noticeable. We also share similar personalities that, I believe, drew us closer together. Although that was not always the case for at least one instance that I remember.

It was during Easter week, undoubtedly the most colorful holiday in Greece.

During Holy Week, people gather in church to follow the passion of Christ.

The forty-day fasting continues until Easter Sunday, but on Monday, the first day of Holy Week, the fasting becomes strict. In church, scriptures about the life of Christ and the apostles are read on this day.

Starting Tuesday, homemakers begin the preparation of koulourakia and other sweets.

In church, scriptures were read about the last supper.

On Wednesday, the anticipation started building, especially for children because the exciting days were coming. In church, the priests anoint the faithful with holy water.

The housewives continue the preparation for the big feast and children help to dye the eggs red, to symbolize the blood of Christ. Women and young girls spend most of the day in the church to decorate the epitaphios, the bier of Christ, with garlands of white and purple flowers; in preparation to receive the body of Christ the next morning. In the evening, the priest recites the twelve gospels while a giant cross with an image of Christ nailed to it, towers in the middle of the church. Friday is the day of mourning.

The drama of the death of Christ is followed with great

devoutness. Businesses close their doors and flags are flown at half-mast. For the love of Christ, who was given vinegar to drink, sweet things are not eaten, out of respect. Also, no one should use a hammer, nails or a saw on this day. In the morning, the body of Christ is taken down from the cross and placed on the epitaphios. That evening, the procession of the epitaphios, representing the funeral of Christ begins. A band playing solemn music precedes the procession followed by a choir singing hymns. Behind them the cantors, the clergy, women bearing myrrh oil and altar boys carrying the liturgical fans. The epitaphios follows and behind it, thousands of the faithful sing hymns.

The parade in the streets continues for several hours. All along the way, bystanders throw flowers on the passing bier of Christ and hold lit candles in their hands.

Early on Saturday morning, the women start to prepare the feast for midnight; a time when the fasting ends.

Since there is not enough space inside the church for the masses of people, the faithful gather outside a few hours before midnight. If a person attends church services once a year, this is that day.

By now people are wary of the extensive services and the extended fast. They are anxious for the grand celebration of the midnight and for the feast waiting for them at home.

The mass reaches its pinnacle at midnight. This is the most significant event in Christianity: The resurrection of Christ.

When the priest lights his candle and calls on everyone to receive the light of Christ and proclaims Christos Anesti, Christ has risen, is when the pandemonium erupts. The faithful rush toward the priest, extending their arms, to light their candles. At the same time, loud and colorful pyrotechnics light the sky.

Firecrackers, church bells, ship sirens, and car horns create a deafening atmosphere. There are shouts of joy amidst the smoke and fire from the explosives that provoke an astonishing excitement. There is embracing and smiles, even those who have created bitterness among themselves, now is the time to forget their hatred.

It is a time that the world stands still in the name of compassion and love.

When the mass is over, shortly after midnight, multitudes of people take to the streets, headed for their homes. The dark streets are now filled with endless lines of moving candlelights. When they reach home, a feast awaits them to celebrate the ending of fasting.

On Easter Sunday the celebration continues. The day begins with the traditional roasting of the lamb on the spit and ends with dances, food and wine.

I remember the Easter week when I was eight years old. I wanted to buy firecrackers for Saturday's celebration, but I had no money.

In the afternoons, between lunch and dinner, my father used to take a break. He would put a chair in front of the door, meaning that the taverna was closed.

Sometimes he walked to the beach, sat on the sand and soaked his feet in the seawater. Other times he went to the coffee shop, a few doors from the taverna, to play cards or backgammon for a couple of hours.

It was the Thursday of the Easter week when I decided to go to the taverna. My little sister was sitting on the chair by the door as if she was taverna's guardian. As I passed her chair and entered the store, I asked my sister to look out for our father and to let me know if he was coming. I just wanted to find a couple of drachmas, enough for a few firecrackers. I remember the eerie quietness as I was walking deeper into the narrow room. I stood behind the table my father used as a counter. A few moments went by. I build up my courage and open the wooden drawer where my father kept his money. The impulse to have a few noisemakers, to be a part of the explosive ambiance on Saturday night, overcame the sweat on my forehead and the guilty feelings in my heart. Soon after I opened the drawer, obscure darkness covered the entire room. I looked up and saw my father standing by the door. My father was a man of few words – he mostly expressed his feelings with facial expressions. That particular moment is frozen in time for me. I cannot forget those eyes spitting fire. My father disdained hypocrisy and dishonesty. Later in life, I will always remember that moment, feeling that I was one of those who he despised. As he walked toward me, I felt like begging and crying, but I knew that was not going to work. The urge to escape his wrath overcame all other emotions. In a bold move of desperation, I crawled under the table and ran out. On my way out I heard his voice, explosive and deafening, and I ran for cover.

On my way out, I looked at my sister - "How could you do this to me?"

Later in life, she told me that when she saw our father walking back, about half a block away, she was speechless because she knew I was doing something wrong. She tried to say something but panicked, and no voice came out of her mouth. Before she could react, my father was standing by the door. "It took you too long, you are not cut out for that job," she said. She was four-years-old after-all.

I ran home for safety. I thought of begging my mother to protect me, but I knew at this point that no one was willing to stand against my father. I looked behind me, down the long street, I saw my oldest brother coming. I knew that my dad sent him after me. I ran through the backyard of the house, wearing a pair of shorts and a white T-shirt, towards my only escape route; my beloved sea. It was late afternoon. The radiant sun ahead of me was about to leap into the blue water.

My brother called me, to go back, but there was no point of return to my father's wrath and to the place of my shamefulness.

My brother was a great swimmer and loved water sports. He ran into the house to get the flippers he used for spear-gun fishing and came after me. Further, I went to evade him, so far that I reached the dreadful black shaded strip of the water. Growing up by the sea, and looking beyond the shallow waters, there was that mysterious dark line on top of the water. I've always wondered about that distant dark strip and thought that it was a point of no return – a place of shaded unknown sea creatures. As I reached the dark waters, my heart drummed on my chest. The sensation that some creature will pull me underneath the water made me swim faster. Beyond the dark shaded waters, which was merely the reflection of sea plants, there was my blue water again. At this point, I could hardly see the people on the beach. My brother had given up the chase; he thought it was wise to wait out by the beach. He figured that I had to go back sometime. My arms were getting tired as I swam closed to the tilting sun and slowly circled the beach-front aiming for the city's harbor. By the time I reached the harbor, it was getting darker and the water was cold. When I finally lifted myself out of the waters, the street lights had come on. My fingers were wrinkled from being in the water for so long, and the sea breeze was penetrating my body. I walked towards the taverna, which was a short distance from the port.

My parents were preparing for the evening customers. My mom saw me and came outside. "What did you do?" she asked, "Your father is mad."

I was shivering as my wet clothes were drying on my body. She took off her jacket and wrapped it around me. Then she begged all the saints and Mother Mary to protect me, like any good Greek mother would do, and told me that if my father saw me, he would kill me. I said, "mom, I am dying here, and you are telling me that dad would kill me."

She smiled, "Go home before you catch pneumonia." She then looked at me with eyes full of love and said to me, "When are you going to learn? You always get into trouble!"

I ran home and changed my clothes. I waited around the house. I was hungry but did not dare to go to the taverna. Finally, I fell asleep, exhausted from the day's events. I woke up to the morning sun. I was surprised. I thought I would be waking up with my father's wrath. I tiptoed to his room and peeked inside. He had gone to work already. My father, the wise man, figured that I had gotten enough punishment for the day.

I walked outside into our yard. My mother was feeding the chickens. She looked at me and smiled. "Come," she said, "I'll make you breakfast."

As I was eating, she looked at me with an expression of true love – an expression that is engraved in my brain to identify the trueness of love. "Your father was not happy last night. He is waiting to talk to you in the taverna," she said. The thought of facing my father was not pleasant. I was afraid I had disappointed him. The only thing he told me later that day was, "Son, if you need money to buy things, just ask"

That was a day full of great lessons.

"When are you going to use those brains in that head of yours?" my mother asked.

"Soon, Mama," I said.

The years went by in the small town, and when I was out of grammar school, my father decided it was time for us to go to Athens to continue our education. In our preparation to go we had to give away our dog, Jack, but every time we gave him to someone he always returned home to us. My uncle and my oldest brother drove him to a small village, about two hours away and left him with a family that they knew would take care of him.

A couple of days later I was sitting with my brothers outside the house, and suddenly we saw Jack coming back. He seemed tired as if he had walked for several hours. The black German Shepherd started to wag his tail and jump as he saw us. He began to run toward us. I heard the brakes screeching on the asphalt and then saw the dog being crushed under the wheels of the truck. "Stop!" I screamed as I ran towards the accident. But it was too late. In his excitement to get to us, Jack did not see the truck coming.

I stayed up crying that night.

The memory of our loyal friend who protected us during our childhood was gone but never to be forgotten. Jack was a big part growing up and despite the sadness of that moment, my childhood was full of love. Unconditional love.

As I look back through hundreds of names of those whom I have admired, to find the heroes that shape my thoughts, I always end up with the same two people.

A man and a woman.

The man stood tall, powerful and proud. In every one of his steps, the earth creaked under his feet. His eyes possessed the pride of an eagle and the wisdom of an owl.

The woman stood firm, undaunted. The body was full of dynamic energy. Her heart a river of endless love. They have taught me great lessons, allowed me to be unconventional and schooled me to accept all people as equals.

My father, the Cretan from where the proudest of Greeks come. My mother the Corinthian, where the most aristocratic families were groomed.

My Parents

5

THE ROOTS

My parents arrived at the crossroads of my destiny from different social backgrounds.

The area of Sfakia is in the southwest part of the island of Crete. The Cretans are notorious for their pride and braveness. Family honor takes precedence among these courageous men and brave women. Sfakia is where my great-grandfather was born, in a family of twelve brothers and one sister. There is a story told throughout the generations about this sister.

In the early nineteen-hundreds, during the fighting for independence from the Turks, the pasha in charge of the Turkish army in Chania, wanted the beautiful sister to be a part of his harem collection of young girls. She was at the tender age of sixteen.

At the dawn of that fateful day, a handful of Turkish soldiers broke into the family home and captured her. The neighborhood was awakened by the panicking screaming of the young girl as she was being dragged out of her house and on to the narrow dirt road.

Many of her brothers ran to her rescue and met the pasha's soldiers determined to save their sister. The fighting was intense; some soldiers fell to their death and a few of the Cretan men were injured. A light rain began to fall from the nebulous sky; some men rolled around the bloody wet dirt. More soldiers came. The brutal scenery of men savagely slitting each other's flesh and the uproar of agonizing screams continued.

The young girl, horrified in the midst the bloodshed and fear of being violated, begged for her brothers not to let her be taken.

Some of her brothers broke between the soldiers and circled their sister.

Lifeless bodies mounted on the wet dirt of the narrow street. The sister knew that her brothers would die trying to save her. To spare her brothers and herself of being violated by the oppressors, she held the knife of one of the brothers against her heart. "Please brother, help me die." As the knife penetrated her heart, she whispered, "Thank you, brother, for letting me die free."

Her beautiful body fell on the bloody mud. The brothers broke away and fled from the area and scattered to nearby villages, leaving behind the body of two brothers and several dead soldiers. They fled on foot, running throughout the rugged country going north towards the town of Chania. They stayed for a while in the village of Mouzoura, then scattered to other surrounding villages; they knew that the Turkish soldiers would be looking for them.

One of those brothers was my great-grandfather. Running for safety, he separated from his family and ended up in the village of Halepa. There he stayed for the rest of his life. A few years after the legendary event, he married and had seven children. One of his sons was my grandfather, Eleftherios, who married my grandmother, Eleni, and had eleven children.

Their youngest son, Stefanos, was born in 1908. His rebellious nature forced him to travel to places away from Crete. His travels brought him to Athens. He spent some time in Athens working odd jobs. Then he was called for his military duty and was stationed at the military base in Corinth.

My maternal great-grandparents were born in Matesi of Andritsena. As a young couple, they operated a traveler's station. Their place provided room and food for travelers, as well as services and stabling for horses and mules. Their business allowed them to raise their four children, all boys, in a pleasant environment.

When the boys came of age, they moved to Nikea, a suburb of Piraeus and started a shoe sales and repairs business. Because of the dishonesty of one of the brothers who spent the business money for his entertainment, the other three brothers sold the company and moved back to the Corinthian province. They settled in the village of Goura, a place in the northern mountains of Corinthia.

Most of the residents of that village were from aristocratic families. One of the brothers, Andreas, fell in love with Sofia. However, Sofia's noble family was not about to accept a commoner into their family. In the name of love, Sofia left the wealth of her family behind and eloped with Andreas to the beach-town of Kiato. There my grandparents were married and had five children: four boys and one girl named Anastasia. A few years later my grandfather opened a small taverna. My grandparents worked hard trying to provide for their family during those difficult years.

Kiato has always been one of the tourists favored destination. It was a favorite destination for Stefanos as well. Every time he took a leave from his military base in Corinth, he would visit Kiato, a short distance away. On one of his visits to Kiato, Stefanos saw Anastasia swimming in the sea. After that day his visits to Kiato became more frequent.

Stefanos and Anastasia fell in love and they got married. The year was 1942.

Their five children grew up in Kiato and were raised by the mother's family.

My maternal grandfather passed just before I was born. Our grandmother and our four uncles were a big part of our childhood.

The most striking memories I have from all of my uncles is how respectful they were to their mother and how they made sure that she had anything she wanted. My favorite uncle was Panagiotis, he had polio and walked with a cane, despite that handicap he was the most active. He was one of the nicest persons I had known in my life. Besides, being the president of the local team named Pelopas, he took me to all the soccer games.

Nikos Ligidakis

My parental grandparents, Eleftherios and Eleni.

My maternal grandparents, Andreas and Sofia.

6

A DREADFUL STEP

When I was a child, I've always daydreamed of travel. At times, standing by the railroad tracks at the edge of the city or by the bus stop, I had the urge to see the world beyond my little town. Watching the trains laboring away and the buses taking passengers to various destinations, the thought of going aboard was enough to put a smile on my face. I would imagine being in a fictional place, participating in multiple activities; playing soccer in a stadium full of fans or helping people in poverty-stricken countries. I wanted to see everything from green mountains, vast oceans and scorched sands of deserts; to meet people of different cultures and to experience actual life-changing moments. At those moments, between daydreaming and reality, I was caught in a tormented state of mind; leaving Kiato was inconceivable. My beloved town seemed to be at the edge of the earth. I was confident that there was nothing like it anywhere else. The beautiful beach, the excitement of the agora, the active sunrises and mellow sunsets, the bluest of seas, the kindness of the people, the endless fruit groves. And there was my family and my friends, and the legendary soccer games on Sundays. Leaving all of that behind was a terrifying thought.

These were the thoughts of a happy child with a conflicted mind, until traveling became a reality.

After my elementary education I had to move to Athens, "to be educated," dad said, and on I went for the long trip. My daunting thoughts about leaving my beloved town for unknown destinations turned to distressed emotions.

The trip seemed endless. At first, the old bus drove between the sea and the lush greenery and then climbed on to a dangerously narrow road at the edge of the mountain. As the bus kept taking sharp turns above the shifting scenery of sea and canyons, I felt dizzy. My mother sitting next to me handed me a paper bag.

I looked at her with confusion, "Just in case you need it, son," she said. When my breakfast backed up to my throat, I figured out what to do with that paper bag. As the bus moved downwards from the mountain road into the populated cities and closer to our destination, my uneasiness intensified. My mother sensed my anxiety and held my hand. Her smile was reassuring; she knew the world beyond our small city well enough to guide me through it. The absolute trust I felt for my mother relaxed my senses.

As we moved farther from the familiarity of my beloved town, a bit of sadness covered my heart. The unknown was exciting and uncertain, but the familiar was comforting and reassuring. I had an uneasy feeling that the days of my carefree childhood were over.

I was worried about the friendliness of the people in the big city, and about the possibility that the salty breeze from the sea, the scent of the mountain thyme, the white flowers on the almond trees, my favorite fig tree, and the aroma of jasmine will slowly fade in my memory.

Finally, driving through streets with myriads of people and hordes of cars, we arrived at our destination. As I stepped down from the old bus, there were deafening noises, tall buildings and dense air.

I stood against the wall of the bus station building, looking with amazement at the alarming disturbances of the big city. The sky seemed dark and the people on the streets unfriendly. The smell of different foods mixed with the polluted air brought me an unpleasant, yet mysterious feeling. A voice inside me was telling me to go back. There was an impulsive feeling that I should not to take the first step towards the big city.

I saw my mother's hand extended towards my hand. I held on to her hand and stepped toward the madness of the big city. The step was cold and insecure. My legs were trembling, and my bright smile became a severe look. My innocent heart started beating faster as I walked into the midst of that human jungle.

The unknown was undoubtedly fascinating.

I watched the merchants arguing on the streets for a few drachmas. The young were running, and the old were strolling. Lovers held hands. People seemed to argue, salespeople pestered consumers to visit their stores, and strangely dressed women invited men into their homes. There were street merchants and magicians doing tricks with cards and taking people's money. My young mind was overwhelmed, confused and fascinated.

As we walked on the streets and people looked at me, I felt that they were mocking me; "Welcome to Athens kid. This is not one of the magical places you imagined."

My mother guided me to the train station. Only this wasn't the train I was accustomed too. The station was underground, and the train was fast and was running on electricity. How amazing, I thought, an electric train! As we left the city's havoc and arrived in the suburbs, things seemed a little different. Children were playing on the streets; there were parks and trees, small quaint shops, outdoor cafes and the people seemed relaxed.

Amidst the different surroundings of the big city, my innocent mind was clouded with questions. The beautiful world I've pictured was now an illusion. Eventually, I understood that my innocent mind had to strengthen to survive the city's madness. I was thirteen years old when I took that long trip. Although I was naive about the world beyond my little town, I was blessed with a skillful mind. I moved to Athens because I was accepted to a college to study engineering.

My mother left me with my aunt to take care of me. When it was time for my mom to go back to Kiato, I walked with her to the train station to say goodbye. She hugged me for several minutes, "We'll be back, son. I promise." I felt safe because my mom always kept her promises. "I'll be fine, mom. Don't worry." I remember that warm motherly embrace that always, in a time of doubt took me to secure space.

When I took the metro to the other side of town, where my school was, I had to act like a grown up. I had to leave that little boy from the small town behind and become a young man. I wanted to be a part of this grownup social makeup. I wanted to be involved with excessive arguments at the outdoor cafes and react to the radical voices about social issues. During my college years, I saw my friends acting impulsively about political idealism and also having envious desires for the lifestyles of the rich and famous.

We would argue vigorously for good without understanding what was bad. The importance of notoriety had taken over the interest of substance.

My school was never the same; a car planet replaced my

blue sea. My classes were more complicated. I wondered if my professors knew that it was difficult for my young mind to comprehend subjects like algebra and physics. Girls looked different somehow, and boys did not seem innocent anymore. Sports were more fun than homework. Hanging around with friends kicking the soccer ball was more important than any classroom. Staying out late was better than getting up early. Looking good was more important than feeling good.

Eventually, my mother and some of my siblings came to Athens and we moved to our small home in Kallithea, a place which eventually became my other beloved neighborhood. It was in that home that defined genuine love for me.

I remember the darkness and the light.

There were several tall trees on my way home. On one spot the treetops covered the moonlight and created absolute darkness. When I stepped into that dark section, my emotions suddenly changed. An urgency to run out of the darkness overcame my senses. I quickened my steps, feeling that someone was behind me, chasing me. After a few steps into the lighted section of the street, I felt silly. A silly boy, afraid of the darkness. But the fact that I knew my family was waiting to greet me and hug me with love as soon as I walked into our little house made every fear and insecurity vanish.

I was fortunate enough to experience the warmth of love.

My childhood was amazing, filled with beautiful experiences. It was not the toys or the riches, because we didn't have any. It was the love.

The unconditional love.

With one of my uncles, just before the journey to Athens.

7

PARALLEL UNIVERSE

Now, when I walk down on Perivolion Street everything seemed so different. The electric train station and the college I attended were the only strong reminiscence of the past. There were many more homes built on my street and a tall building towered in the little fields where we use to play soccer.

Beyond the small iron gate, the yard of our old home, the place where we lived over thirty years ago seemed so tiny now. The twisting iron stairway leading to the flat rooftop where we spent many summers nights sleeping was rusty from the passing of time. The four small homes where families once lived are now deserted. I pushed the door open and entered my old home. My initial reaction was disbelief; It was impossible to imagine that we had lived in these two small rooms.

It reminded me of the time when my family first moved to Athens. I was the first one to move at the age of thirteen. I stayed with my aunt in the suburb of Patissia. It was difficult to accept the big city life as my home. I felt misplaced in the commotion of the big city, especially when I was told that I had to take the electric train to go to school. My school in Kiato was a walk away and no people were running in the shadows of the tall buildings or millions of cars jamming the streets.

I was still tormented by the tumultuous life in the city a semester later and relieved when my mother and siblings moved to Athens, so we could all be together. We found this little unit to stay in Kallithea because it was close to my school. My father had stayed back in Kiato to work and provide for us. We always looked forward to going back to Kiato on holidays and in the summertime to see our dad.

I stood in amazement in the middle of that tiny area we used to call home. A small kitchen shared the same space with a table and a bed. The other room containing two beds and was equally short of space.

For a moment I thought maybe I was in the wrong place. But as I felt the wall shaking and the noise of the fast-moving electric train passing right next to the back wall of the house, it brought me back to reality; this was the right place.

Strangely now, I felt no connection to this place other than it was our home for a while. To me, a home was a place where I could run along with my leaping buddy Jack, our German Sheppard, through the trees and flowers and jump into waters of the blue sea. A place where the sea breeze drifted through the windows while taking my afternoon nap.

I walked out in the yard. It was amazing that this neighborhood had changed so much. I tried to leave the picture intact as it was thirty years ago; the street we played on, the field where we kicked around the soccer ball. Our mother, chasing us into the house to do our homework. Children gathered around the ice cream truck, homemakers picking vegetables and fruits from the open truck of the produce man to prepare dinner. Groups of people seating out in the yards in the evening to talk. I was torn between romanticism and realism; I wanted the neighborhood to be the same as when I left.

The bright sun tilted to the western horizon. I saw Dimitris, the son of the plaster maker, and my teammate from our local soccer team. He was still there, creating art for home decorating. I talked with him for a while, reminiscing about the old days and our friends. Life had changed and become more complicated for all of us.

Walking back to my car, familiar voices of Greek singers lamenting about love and life's struggles dispersed from inside the homes. Along the narrow street, there were still jasmine, white lilies and violets on balconies, basil and tomatoes in the backyards, and aromas of cooked foods, coming out from the windows.

At the end of the street in the coffee shops, people gathered to watch soccer games. I remembered the passionate fans divided between their teams. Temporary animosity would fill the air, the fans whose team lost they seemed always to blame the referee. Others would have coffee or ice cream while arguing about politics.

I had a strong urge to drive to Kiato, to my childhood grounds. I got in my car and as I was driving there, I thought about all the sacrifices my parents had made. My mother had moved away from my father and the town that she grew up in to take care of her children. My dad stayed behind to labor alone, day and night in the taverna, so his five children could go to school and have food to eat.

My mother stayed in Athens with us during the school season and we went to Kiato the rest of the time. My parents were not divorced, or anything like that, this kind of a thing was foreign to the people back then, they stuck together no matter the circumstances. On my way to Kiato, I imagined my father riding a bus on his way to Athens, to solve the problems of his teenage children or to take care of those who were sick. I remember he was always there to lecture us or to comfort us.

As I drove into Kiato, I pulled around the house we had grown up. Everything was so different here as well. By the beach, there were many coffee shops and tavernas. The backyard which once was linked to the sea was now fenced in and blocked, making way for the traffic of people and cars. I went to my old school and glanced into the schoolyard. The same trees were there. It was empty because of summer break, but I could swear I heard the voices of children playing. I walked across the street to the beautiful church of Agia Sotira and from there I could see the spot where my father's taverna used to be. I imagined my parents working; my father arriving in the morning to prepare and my mother soon joining him. Sometimes she sat at the long table snapping pea pods or cleaning lentils and beans. By noon the seats were full of people with more waiting to be seated. The smells of food, the aroma of wine, the buzzing of the people inside the small taverna, recreated the magical atmosphere in my mind.

My father dished out the foods. My mother helped serve and my little brother, Giorgos, always helped as well. I remember that little boy that everyone loved, rushing from table to table. My father was mostly serious. My mother was the one always ready to humor the customers. Then, after the rush of the day and awaiting the evening crowd, the taverna would close for a few hours. Sometimes my father walked by the sea, and my mother went home to finish household chores. I turned my head and looked towards the street which linked to the sea. I imagined the tall man with his tired walk and the serious look on his face coming back to the taverna to prepare for the evening customers. Then I looked in the other direction to see the energetic medium-built body strolling towards the taverna. I looked back and forth in both directions and realized that neither my father nor my mother would be coming back to open the taverna. The aromas of my father's cooking, which people drove for miles around to taste, would never fill the air again.

I felt sadness swelling inside my throat thinking about their absence in my life. I closed my eyes to keep the tears from pouring out. I sealed my lips to prevent from calling their names. I miss them so; I wish they were here, so I could tell them that. I only hope they know how much I appreciated all they did for their children.

I shook my head in amazement. Make your life an example; what a beautiful and positive way to relay a message to the ones you love. Through all my years of traveling from one end of the world to another, they were with me. On every line of their letters, I read their pain. Every sound of their voices missing me still rings in my ears; "Come back. Come home." I would not listen. I wanted to surprise them by saving enough money and building a little home in Kiato, so they could spend their old days together in the place where they had the best memories of their lives.

But things do not always work out the way we plan. My travels throughout the world continued, and dreams were put on hold. The man who, after years of hard work, still stood with a commanding presence, but his walk now was tiresome. The woman with the courage and the love still reflecting on her face, but her step was painful because of her permanently swollen legs. Only then did I realize that the years had gone by without fulfilling my dreams. A lesson that I learned too late;

we must go after our dreams and make them into a reality. I never heard my parents complain about life, and I do not remember any arguments between them. I never noticed them being selfish. They were always giving. They were still caring. I hardly knew what my parents liked because they never told us. I don't think I even saw them go to a movie. My father rode an old bike. My mother walked everywhere. But their wisdom of life was beyond any ordinary person I have ever known. They made me understand that what makes heroes is the unselfishness of sacrificing themselves to spread kindness to the ones you love.

Nikos Ligidakis

With my brothers and sister, growing up in Kiato.

8

THE BICYCLE

When I was a little boy, I marveled at the perfection of the machinery in front of my eyes. Its body was made of steel and the spokes holding the wheels were strong enough to withstand the giant's weight. The handlebars extended their arms into a man's fists, ratchet wheels were attached to the big wheels, bonded with a chain, and there was a leather seat for the comfort of the rider. All a man had to do was push on the rubber tips of the pedals with his feet and on it went. The lucky rider weaved throughout the narrow streets and climbed down the hills. I was mesmerized by such a creation.

What ingenious brain had thought of such a thing? By the time I was three, I had found myself staring at that black beauty resting against the white wall of our house. I felt an emptiness when it was not there. Now I was five and able to sit on the leather seat, the tips of my toes touching the rubber pedals, I felt as if I was sitting on a hill, high above the ground. At six, in my attempt to ride the bike, I found myself face-down on the side of the dirt road, with my knee skinned, blood running down my leg, my elbow was numb, and my face landed near horse droppings. My brain was spinning fast for answers. What story was I going to tell the giant?

My head was stuffed with the awful smell of manure and overwhelmed with dreaded guilt.

Now that I had destroyed the bicycle, the giant would have to walk to work. Fear overcame me. I was certain that he was not going to be happy.

Everyone was taking their nap, except for my friend, Kostas, who lived next door. He was a little bigger than me; he was eight years old. He came over to help me.

We picked the bicycle off the ground. He told me to squeeze the front wheels between my knees, "Push with me," he said, and after a few squeaky noises, the handlebars were straightened up. We cleaned up the dirt off the bicycle; brushed the dry grass stuck in the wheels and back to the white wall we rolled it.

I looked at Kostas walking back to his house and I smile because I was very fortunate to have good friends like him, to help me in a time of crisis.

I glanced back. The bicycle was standing against the wall like it was an hour ago. From the passing of time, the bicycle was now much older; the black paint was fading, the tires warned out, and the leather seat was turning to gray.

I heard my dad waking up and washing his face; soon he would step out into the yard on his way to ride the bicycle to work.

He would probably notice my scratched knee and shake his head. If he feels like it, he will crack a smile, thinking about what I have been up to again. He was used to the sight of me with scratches and cuts, being kicked by a horse, hitting my head on a rock while diving into the sea, or from skidding into the street while chasing the soccer ball.

He had told me once, in his profound voice, that I was not to touch the bicycle without his permission.

And what he said was the law of the land.

My dad came out of the house, looked at the bike, looked back at me, and smiled.

He pedaled the bicycle away, turned the corner of the narrow street, and I dreamed of the day that I could take that turn just like him.

I was a bit older now; I could reach and turn the pedals. I practice, holding onto the wall. I let go, and after a few meters, I was on the ground with the bicycle resting on top of me.

Again and again, I tried. Again and again, I fell.

I wondered why the bicycle did not stand on its two wheels when I am on it. It looks so easy when big people do it.

Every time my dad walked to his bicycle, he looked at me and shook his head.

I wonder if he knew what I was up to while he was taking his nap? When he walked into the house to take his nap, he asked me to watch the bicycle. I was baffled by his mocking voice and mysterious smile. Of course, he knew. I didn't let that smile fool me.

But I couldn't resist, when I heard his snoring, out I went to ride in the afternoon where there was no other sound except for the annoying locusts. I could now ride a few meters without falling, the front wheel shook, but I managed to stay on it.

I held onto a tree, onto a wall and let go of another tree, into another wall.

Every time I rode the bike, I went a little farther, and I was on top of the world when I was able to ride into the streets.

The months unfolded and further, I rode, up to the hills. I climbed and weaved between the trees. I even went into the streets filled with car traffic.

I rang the bell when someone was in my way. I rang the bell when I saw a goat or a mule. But, I always got back in time to catch my breath, wash the sweat off my face and pretend that I was playing in the yard.

The afternoons that he did not take his nap and the bicycle was not there; I felt lonely.

I walk the streets to see the bicycle, but when the giant saw me, he frowned his brows and reminded me that I should be home taking my nap, and so I ran home.

You may disobey the prime minister, the archbishop, the teacher, or the policemen, but you must never disobey your father, well, except in the afternoons when he takes his nap and will never know if you were disobedient.

Soon that bicycle was entirely under my control. I was weaving through traffic, cutting in front of people; I could hear the old people curse between their teeth.

"Damn youth! What is becoming of this world?"

My friend, Kostas, had his bicycle as well. Sometimes we rode together, racing on the streets, going to the beach for a dip in the sea, eating grapes and oranges as we passed the grapevines and the orchards, sharing riding tricks: "Look, no hands!" "Look, I am standing on the seat!" "Look, my foot is on the handlebars!"

A heartrending lament woke up the neighborhood one afternoon; it was coming from Kostas' house. His mother was frantic, crying, screaming his name.

Earlier that afternoon Kostas rode his bicycle onto a hill and never rode back home again. He was carried back.

On his way up the hill, a truck was speeding down, out of control without brakes. Kostas panicked, turned his bike into a field on the side of the road and down to the ground he went with great force, the back of his head hit a big rock.

They took him to the hospital, but it was no use. A hemorrhage, they said, inside his head. The neighborhood and the town mourned for my friend. It was a great tragedy.

Even God-fearing folks had questions. "How could God take a child?" I've heard some saying.

My father pointed his finger at my face, "See what happens when you don't listen?"

Every time I looked at my friend's yard, there was a tightening in my heart; I knew he was never coming out to play with me again.

Occasionally, his mother, dressed in black, step into the yard and looked around as if she were searching for her boy. The old black bicycle stood against the wall. I could not go near it for weeks – since that dreadful day. But, eventually, I could not resist. Every time my father walked to the bicycle, he glanced at me with a suspicious look. I turned my face the other way.

How does he know? I was wondered.

When I took the bike, I was always back in time, except for the day that the back tire went flat. I was far from the house and had to go back dragging the bicycle; it was a long, dreadful walk. I peeked from the corner of the street and there he was, waiting outside the house, hands crossed on his chest. I took a deep breath and worked up the courage to face him.

"A flat tire," I said.

"Hmmm," he growled. Cold sweat ran down my entire body.

"You want to be killed like Kostas," he said. "Why are you not listening?"

He walked away, angry and disgusted with me. He would

not smile anymore; he just looked at me and frowned.

"Do not touch that bicycle," he would say every so often, "I know what you are up to."

Sometimes I walked to the bicycle, sat on the leather seat, but jump off at the slightest sound coming from inside the house, and I didn't go near it if I didn't hear the giant snoring.

One afternoon, I felt overwhelmed. I rolled the bike down the street, between the trees and along the beach-front. I rode it with the crisp breeze on my face, running free.

Tears ran down my face, tears and sweat, and I rode, faster than the cars, faster than anything that moved. I stopped at the end of the town, by the butcher house; the smell of blood and butchered animals nauseated me. It reminded me of my friend and reminded me of my dead body if I was not back in time.

My dad walked out of the house he looked at me with suspicion, shook his head, sat on the doorstep and called me over.

He put his arm around me. "I know what you've been up to. I want you to have fun and a nice life but, my priority is your safety. Soon you will grow up and there will be plenty of time to do whatever you want, but for now, you have to listen. This is the last time."

I never rode that bicycle again.

Nikos Ligidakis

My dad and his bicycle. With Mr. Pitinis

9

VISIONS

Beyond the large glass window, the rain waters were pounding on the sidewalk. Thunder and lightning struck again, opening the skies to flood the streets inexhaustibly. The heavy rain was an unusual phenomenon in Phoenix, Arizona and I wanted to enjoy every moment of that downpour. I felt overwhelmed with emotion as I threw myself back into my chair. The rain does that to me; it provokes perplexed emotions. Images of faraway sun-drenched places ran through my mind; Santorini, Milos, Nafplion. How I wished to be there.

"Come back... come back." The seductive voice of my motherland was calling me again. The same voice that haunted me throughout the decades, following me in my travels around the world. A melancholic feeling was tormenting my soul once again.

Wherever I go, wherever I stay, I hold Greece between each layer of my heart.

In days like this, she is more enticing than ever, like a beautiful woman, one who knows how to be seductive.

My beloved land loves to get drenched in the rain and to be caressed by the sun. She hides nothing, she cries and she laughs, she is fragrance, refreshing and eternal.

Every time I hear her voice, my life's downfalls and the countries I have seen, all float across my mind like clouds, then scatter and vanish to the far horizon.

Only, her voice stays in my mind like a beehive full of workers, drones, and honey.

How can I forget so many emotions, so many feelings, and so many lessons?

There is a joy to watch the first rainfall turning the scorching earth's harshness into a delicate yet robust, earthy fragrance. I remember as a young child I loved to walk in the rain. Under the raindrops I felt a mystical sweet feeling as if I was in a peaceful, barren universe. It was an inexplicable feeling of nature's warm and wet embrace. It is this mysterious feeling that makes the rain so incredibly romantic.

I remember, as a child, what I loved most was the anticipation of rain's intensity. At first, there was the gloominess of the dark clouds in the sky, then thunder and lightning frighten the birds, determined to find shelter. I recall the slow rhythmic fall of raindrops on our tile roof and walking out of the house. As the rain intensified and moistened my clothes, I walked back to our home and sat by the burning fire in our fireplace. Besides the rain, I love fireplaces. When I close my eyes and think about the crackling wood and the intensity of the fire flames, great memories from my childhood awaken inside of me. The wonderful times sitting around the fireplace with our grandmother telling us stories; moments of boundless charm. It was one of the night's when grandmother had gathered the children around the fireplace that the unimaginable happened. We were toasting bread and roasting chestnuts. Grandmother was taking us to faraway places with her stories about dragons and princesses. On top of the fireplace was a ledge where my mother stored various items. Suddenly, a bottle of alcohol fell from the shelf. It sounded like an explosive device as it broke right in front of me. I was not even three years old. I do not remember panic or screams. All I remember was that my body was on fire. Before anyone realized what had happened, my grandmother, well over eighty years old at the time, threw a blanket over me. The old thin body of hers leaped at me with incredible flexibility; like a tiger to protect her babies. In the blink of an eye, she was carrying me to bed wrapped in a blanket. She covered my body with olive oil, then she compounded a homemade remedy and rubbed it on me, and then she covered my entire body with large leaves and wax paper. My grandmother left my side only to bring back the things necessary to replace the ointments.

I stayed in bed for a few days. I remember just a few things from those days in bed; just like a faded dream. Amidst the vague picture of the room, I remember every small detail of the fireplace, exactly where I was sitting when the fire engulfed on my body. Also, there are vivid memories of opening my eyes and always seeing the faces of either my mother, father, or grandmother. They stood by my bed and assured me that I would be taken care of. Their presence eased my pain. The perception of true love entered in my young heart and planted there forever.

I don't remember much pain. When I was awake, I remember my grandmother running her hand through my hair, talking to me softly and all the pain would disappear. The tragic experience left no scars on my body or my mind. To the contrary, the seething fire of the fireplace has always been one of my favorite places to sit by and write or read. For the years to come, my grandmother, my most beloved person, continued telling us stories around the fireplace. It was as though nothing had happened. That awful experience was forgotten. I can't even think of times that it was mentioned. Because of the love surrounding me, the dreadful experience had become a paradigm of the power of love, rather than a tormenting memory.

My grandmother seemed capable of everything. She had the remarkable energy for her age. She helped with household chores and sometimes she took the children to the agora to buy us clothes or shoes. She was extremely protective of us.

She dressed in black from the time of my grandfather's death. I never met my grandparents from my father's side either, because they also died before my birth. Grandma told us stories about our grandparents, our uncles and about our mother and how she had met our father. She was hesitant at first about my father marrying my mother.

When my father arrived in Kiato, he was a stranger in a town where everyone knew each other well. Traditionally, before anyone joined a family, it was a standard requirement to know the history of the person. My father had no money or a job back then. He spoke very little about himself and very few people knew about his background. But he won people over with his demeanor. He was honest, sincere, and straightforward; there was no reason to doubt what he said. In the end, my grandmother loved him and spoke of him with great respect.

Grandma told us about mother and how beautiful she was at a young age. I could only remember my mother working in the taverna and home. She was a little heavier later in life, after giving birth to five children within six years. We were all thankful for the closeness between us, mainly because we were born a few years apart. I think about mother now and how difficult it must have been for her, especially in the war years. But she never complained. My mother was a remarkably strong woman. I've never known someone so intelligent and courageous at the same time. Mother was nobody's fool. Even though she had little schooling, her mind could add and multiply faster than any calculator and she was a good judge of characters. Her convictions about her family were undoubted and her humor was quick and charming. I think about my grandmother's stories and although I do not remember their exact content, I am certain that her stories have influenced my imagination. Her tales had always seemed to find beauty in adversity.

From the child's fearful burning by the fireplace, which became a memorable experience, to other frightening matters later in life, she seemed to always be there in times of need for support and advice. One of those moments was when I was at the age of fourteen. I was spending the summer in Kiato with my dad and staying in my grandmother's home. Everything that I yearned for was there; the clear blue sea, the endless beach-front, warm days, peaceful nights and that fantastic homemade ice cream. It was one of those hot afternoons that the long beach of Kiato was overcrowded with people seeking a refreshing escape in the seawaters. As usual, I was there with a few of my friends. Often, we took turns using my brother's speargun to catch fish. I came out of the water, lay the speargun a few yards ahead of my friends, sat down to join them while one of the friends went on to try catching some fish. Suddenly, there was a hollow sound and my left leg jolted by an immense force. After the initial shock, I noticed the five-hook spear from the speargun nailed in my leg. It was a few inches away from my stomach and not too far from my heart. I felt no pain at that moment; I was just shocked. I looked up at my speechless friend who was about to dive in the sea with the speargun, and with a terrified expression was trying to explain what had happened. One of my friends unscrewed the speargun shaft from its five-tip trident and two others put my arms around their shoulders, helping me to hop on my way to the hospital.

Beyond the beach, we had to pass the hot asphalt road with the heavy car traffic and get into the neighborhood streets leading to the hospital. It was early afternoon; folks were getting up from their nap. Some of them sitting on their house-fronts, watching six teenagers, one of them with a speargun tip stuck in his lower leg. Some of them offered help; others asked questions; a few men said, "hang in there boy," while women made the sign of the cross and prayed out-loud for Mother Mary to take care of me. I felt embarrassed with all that attention; "Please hurry up, get me out of these streets," I remember thinking. I was also concerned about the damage to my leg. "Was my dream of being a great soccer player over?"

We sat in the marble lobby of the small hospital, waiting for the doctor. My grandmother arrived within minutes after our arrival. I have no idea how she knew. She came over to me, held my head, kissed my forehead and begged Mother Mary to keep me safe. She asked me how I felt. "I am okay grandma, don't worry." Then she turned to the boy who was responsible for shooting the speargun tips into my leg – how did she know who he was? "Are you trying to kill my boy?" was among the things I remember her saying. My friend just bowed his head listening and apologizing.

My mother arrived shortly after my grandmother. She looked at my leg then started to ask us questions. My mother was the diplomat and always wanted to know everything. My father walked into the waiting area a few minutes later. With his presence, that area suddenly became very quiet. I looked at him and wanted to say, "Sorry Dad." He then looked at my friends. They turned their faces away - no one wanted to meet his eyes. He said nothing and went on to see the doctor and make arrangements for my operation. The affection and concern of the people about my well-being seemed to subdue my pain. After the doctor checked my foot, he asked my parents to take me to the town's blacksmith, to cut-off and separate the top of each of the five tips of the trident. The doctor suggested that it would be better for him to remove each tip separately.

On to the streets, we went again; my friends were helping me hop on my right foot, my family following and behind them my other friends. The ten-minute walk became an extravaganza of emotions. People's reactions were overwhelming; "What happened to the boy?" "Is he going to be okay?" and I heard every saint's and, of course, Mother Mary's names mentioned along the way.

When we arrive at the blacksmith, Mr. Katharios looked at the hooks planted in my lower leg just above my ankle. For a few seconds seemed perplexed; for sure he had never faced a similar situation. Eventually, he settled on a plan on how to master this task. He brought out his small round electric saw, gave one of my friends a long pair of pliers and handed my mother a bucket of water and a towel.

The sun was descending on the western horizon when Mr. Katharios turned on his electric saw. I watched the fast-turning round blade coming close to my skin and closed my eyes. I heard instructions given to my friend and mother; "you hold tight the trident," "keep the wet towel on the tips of the trident and against the skin."

I had to look; my curiosity overwhelmed my fear of watching. My friend was holding the trident with the pliers while the blacksmith was cutting of the first tip. At the other end, where the steel entered my leg, my mother held the wet towel to prevent the headed metal from burning my skin. I had to admit; it was an ingenious plan.

My grandmother stood behind the blacksmith, giving him instructions on how not to hurt me. In the end, Mr. Katharios looked at me and smiled. "I hope I don't have to do this again, to anyone. It was an experience," he said.

Back at the hospital, we went. Dr. Mihalopoulos numbed my leg and then removed the hooks one by one.

"You are fortunate this did not break your bones," he said.

I looked at the doctor and shook my head. "I am lucky the spear did not hit anywhere else on my body!" I responded.

My grandmother taught me how not to be afraid of fireplaces, and family and friends turned a traumatic experience into a pleasant memory, and most important my love for the deep, mysterious blue sea remained intact.

A few years after that event, I also discovered that my grandmother's love had a vision. Since I have a difficult time comprehending the supernatural or anything else that I am not able to define, it is difficult to explain what happened the last time I saw her.

I was nineteen-years-old, just before going on a trip abroad. I was staying with my grandmother. She had a lovely home with a colorful garden full of beautiful trees, flowers and vegetables. In the yard, there was also a little chapel where she prayed every day. Her home was as if you were in Shangri-La. On the day before my trip, she called me into her tiny chapel. It was darkened and mysterious in there. The walls were decorated with icons of the saints and a few candles were burning. I remember the eerie feelings vividly while sitting in that uncommon space. My grandmother sat across from me and held my hand. "My son, tomorrow will be the last time I am going to see you," she said.

There was a long pause while I was looking at her. She was full of life even though she was over one hundred-years-old. No one knew her exact age, as was the case with most elders whose birth certificates were lost during the wars.

"What are you saying, grandma?" I asked, "I'll be back to see you soon."

She smiled; that peaceful smile of hers that brightened her entire wrinkled face. "God is calling me and I must go. I have been preparing myself for this. Death is not a bad thing. I am ready to move on to the next life."

"But I will miss you. Life without you is not going to be the same."

"You will not miss me because I will be with you forever."

"Grandmother, I will be back before you know it," I replied.

She told me that I would be gone longer than I thought. She talked about the endless travels throughout my life, and finally that I was going to live in a place far away from Greece. A place beyond the vast ocean where I would get married and have three children. "You are going to live a long and adventurous life." She said. For a moment I thought grandmother had lost her senses, but that was a fleeting thought. I asked her about the girl that I was dating from Holland. She told me that I was not going to make a future with her and she could only see me married in another far away country. She spoke with wisdom, but, despite the great respect I had for her, I had difficulty believing in what she was saying. At the age of nineteen, I did not want to foresee my future. I looked at her. The anemic reflection from the candlelight exposed an incredible image. The candlelight, shadowing her wrinkled face and highlighting the brightness in her eyes, would have made a masterful painting.

She touched my face with her hands; goosebumps ran through my body. She looked at me with love in her eyes and then she kissed me on my forehead.

"Come on. I will make you dinner," she said as she got up, holding my hand.

I didn't go back to Greece after my trip to Holland. After spending a few months in Rotterdam, I went to Venezuela for a while. From there I went to New York, then to Canada, and from there to Osaka, Japan. It is where I got the news that my grandmother had died.

One evening as she was having dinner she choked on a chicken bone. She was taken to the hospital where the doctor operated on her throat to remove the bone. The operation was successful, and the doctor told her that she would be fine. She was in the same hospital where I had been to remove the spear tips from my foot. The same doctor operated on her. Often, I wonder if she was in the same room.

Two days later she called all her children and grandchildren by her bedside. She asked my mother to bring one of my photographs with her. She talked to everyone individually, wishing each a good life and to honor love and humanity. The family visit went on for a few hours. In the end, she placed my picture by her heart. "He is the only one who I will not see for the last time," she said.

Everyone tried to humor her by telling her that she would be okay and that she looked healthy. But after she told everyone her goodbyes, she asked them to leave the room. A few minutes later she passed peacefully.

I remember our conversation in that little chapel and recognize those predictions about my life. It was as if grandmother had written my life story. I often think about that vision of hers, unable to explain it. Since my mind is generally engaged in subjects of realness and reason, I believe her foresight was because of her great love. A love that allowed her to see my happiness and my agonies. It is a far-fetched theory because I will never know for sure. The only thing I know is that I felt a powerful mystifying feeling back in that little chapel which is impossible to forget; a feeling that was created from a love that had a vision.

My Heroes, My Town

10

ALTAR BOY

Grandmother was the one who introduced me to religion. She wanted me to go to Sunday school and to show up at church every Sunday. My mother just went along with grandmother's wishes and my father could care less about religion. Eventually, my grandmother convinced me to be an altar boy.

Along with three other boys, I entered the back quarters of the church. The priest asked us to kiss the icons of a few saints and then he extended the back of his hand for me to kiss. Next, he handed each of us a white vestment, "Put it on and meet me at the altar table," he said pointing to a small dressing room. The somber feeling of the back room, the bizarre idea of kissing icons and the egotistical gesture of someone wanting me to kiss his hand was not a good start to my altar boy introduction. Things did not get any better after that. Standing in the church, full of people, holding a candle and dressed in an annoying white robe, was the most awkward situation I have ever been. And for the next two hours was the worst torture you could put a child through.

When the altar boy ordeal was over, I went back to the taverna and I told my mother that I would kill myself if I had to do it again. My father laughed and said, "one less mouth to feed." Luckily he was joking and being the just father he was he relieved me from that dreadful duty.

My grandmother, bless her soul, took all five of us to the agora and once a year she bought a pair of shoes for each one of us. Our shoes were always a size bigger because our feet were growing too fast. She was a saint of a woman and left behind many impressive memories and lessons which I used as guidance to overcome adversities. Forcing me to be an altar boy was not one of those moments.

My religious practices were behind the church, on a dirt road in front of the beach. It was where I spent most of my waking hours kicking the soccer ball. The soccer field of the town, with the goalposts and the stands, was a sacred place where the real footballers practice and play. In our area, behind the church, we placed two large stones for goalposts and there were no white lines, like the soccer field. We played hard to win and when my team lost, my sleep was disturbed. I remember one game when the score was a tie and, after hours of playing, we decided whoever scores a goal next would be the winner. I was the hero of that game when I score an excellent goal, but the other team's players disputed it, claiming that the ball was outside the stone used as a post. There were heated arguments, shouts and animosity prevailing over friendship. During the heated arguments, one of the opposing team players picked up a heavy stone and threw it at me from point blank. The rock hit me on the back of my head and left me with a big bump. After the bitter feud, it was time to go to my father's taverna and eat. But how would I show up there with a big bump on the back of my head and no hair to hide it. The only option was to protect the back of my head from my father. As we talked, every time he turned, I turned. Finally, he looked at me with curiosity, "What is the matter with you," he asked. "Nothing dad," I answered. "Have you done anything wrong?" He insisted.

"Who me?" I acted surprised.

My father smiled and shook his head. "What does this kid think that I am stupid?" He probably thought.

Luckily there were no customers in the taverna to asked questions about the bump on the back of my head. Somehow, I escaped the taverna with my injury unnoticed and went home to show it to my mother. My grandmother was there and she washed my head with cold water and begged all the saints and Mother Mary to protect me.

"Here we go again with the saints and Mother Mary," I thought to myself.

"Your father will not be happy about this," mother said. But that's how it was then; our parents did not want us fighting on the streets when we should be doing our homework.

Now, reflecting, I remember that my mother seldom went to church just because she had five children running around and the responsibility of helping my dad in the taverna. My father, on the other hand, was an intellectual, logic was his guidance in life.

My father was a progressive thinker, kind of what you call a liberal nowadays but not the character to go to Starbucks and drive a Volvo. First of all, no one knew what Starbucks was back then, and my father rode a bicycle to the taverna.

If there is heaven, my parents are there.

Grandmother would pray every day in her little chapel. She used to tell me, "Pray to Christ, Mother Mary, to the Saints and good things would happen in your life." I remembered looking at the icons of the saints, asking for good things in life, and in exchanged I got to live in a country ruled by George W Bush;

thanks a lot, saints!

Besides soccer my other passion was foosball. I remember, when a teenager in Athens, I had a foosball partner and we tour in various neighborhoods to play foosball with other teams. The rooms where we played were like small arcades with a few pinball machines, foosball tables, and billiards. Playing against the neighborhood's best players was intense. There would be several people hovering around the foosball table to watch the fierce competitions. Most of the people attending were betting on the outcome of the game and all remained silent during the game, only in the end there were cheers and jeers. The money would exchange hands while people tried feverishly to bet on the next game.

The tough games were, most of the time, prolonged since it took a while for each ball to sink into the opposite goal. My teammate and I had very little money to bet, but when we won, we got tips from those who wagered with us. That was my first experience with gambling and my initiation to the adrenaline effect while trying to win. But, again, real football was my passion. It was an injury to my right ankle that turned my life upside down.

Until then everything was fine, I knew what I wanted to do in life, to be a professional football star. The doctor said that the ankle was dislocated. He put it back in place and told me to wait four or five months before I was to kick the ball again. I thought, sure Doc, you have no idea what it's like to watch others run around on the field while I am looking in. It is torture, for a seventeen-year-old future star to be going through it.

It wasn't even three months gone by, my foot felt fine and I ran into the field of dreams. It was in the second half that the ankle gave in again; it swelled and was painful when putting any weight on it. I guess the old doc was right, but a young bull seventeen years of age is blind to the advice because at a young age we know everything and anyone older than twenty-five is brainless and boring.

Well, because I didn't listen to those illogical people, my dreams to be a soccer star were crushed, and I had to live with that regret because I was responsible for betraying my dreams.

The main church in Kiato

11

PASSION

The people came from all directions and poured into the streets of our town in torrential waves. Ordinary folks came from villages and nearby cities; sons and daughters of farmers, workers and storekeepers. They arrived by bus, on motorcycles, in carpools; young and old, willing to raise their voice – the voice of hope. It was election time, the entire country was in a state of excitement, like a great holiday. In our little town, there was incredible energy as well because the "orator" was to arrive in the afternoon. I knew he was coming because, in the early hours of the morning, Kyr-Andreas, the barber walked into my father's taverna, covered father's face with foamy cream and with his sharp, long razor gave my father a good shave. My father did something unusual that day; he closed his taverna. Then in the early afternoon, wearing his Sunday clothes, he headed towards the town's square. There was an enchanted expression on his face. I followed in his footsteps.

Along the way, the people moved slowly on the crowded streets. We passed closed storefronts and empty coffee shops. The car traffic was on hold and the only activity in the city was the movement of people towards the town square.

My father found a spot within the human hordes, I tried to

look around me, but all I could see were human bodies. I was standing by my father's leg when voices ascended from the earth to reach the heavens. A current of excitement waved in the air. I knew the "orator" was out on the balcony, but I could not see him. "Dad, dad, please." I pulled on my father's trousers. He turned his face towards me. I had never seen him so mesmerized. My father lifted me up and set me on his broad shoulders. The balcony was decorated with wreaths and flowers. A large sign hung from the balcony that read, "Victory For The People."

The rooftops and the verandas of the surrounding buildings were packed with human bodies. People were hanging from the trees and the lampposts. They stood on car tops and in the back of trucks.

A sea of flags waved in the summer breeze; signs with messages of hope were lifted high. An electrical charge ran through my little body. My mind was overwhelmed with the magical atmosphere.

The man on the balcony was standing behind a microphone. He lifted his arms and calmly waived to the crowd. He seemed like a giant of a man. Rousing voices returned the greeting. There were tears of excitement in my eyes, and goosebumps on my body. It was a moment of magic, a moment nestled in the safest bank of my memory.

He began to speak and suddenly the voices quieted down, and the crowd stood motionless. The words came out of the megaphone, crisp and infallible.

Periodically, the crowd awakened the heavens with roaring voices. They shouted words of hope and admiration, loud enough to reach the ears of God.

I watched the faces around me; there were smiles on their

lips, hope in their eyes. The man on the balcony spoke about the poor and the needy. I heard the words education and medicine. He mentioned responsibility and children, compassion and elders, in the same sentences. The passion of his words penetrated my heart. He spoke to the workers and the farmers. I heard words of equality and freedom. He said that the rich must care and share, that the poor must have hope and pride.

I don't remember how long the speech went on. To me, it seemed like an eternity. It was a frame of time that long after the crowd had quieted down, long after the confetti was swept from the grounds, long after everyone had returned to their villages, to their homes, the voice of hope had been restrained within the compounds of my soul. The words I heard on that day were transformed into a dream that I know is true. An idea that unites the sentiments of misery and hope in the perpetual triumph of the human spirit.

My Heroes, My Town

12

DEFENSELESS

The blasting sound from the ship's foghorn roared three times. It was time to go. The winch on the ship's deck labored while dragging on the heavy lines from the dock. The vessel pulled away slowly from the pier and out onto the seawaters it went. Tugboats pushed the cargo ship towards the open waters and into the mist it went. As the engine room was ordered to slow ahead, the great propeller penetrated the waters and moved the vessel forward. I stood at the stern for a last look. Beyond the darken skies another city was pulling away. The great propeller accelerated its speed and sent the vessel into the ethereal morning fog and on to the gray ocean. The foghorn roared again and again, like a mournful cry of a misplaced beast, lost in a place composed of water and fog.

The next morning, far away from the docks of Vancouver, the fog had cleared. The floating home of thirty-five seamen was steering full speed ahead, mowing the endless miles of the mysterious world beneath the ocean.

We endured the daily routine as the vessel, a single molecule on the ocean stubbornly propelled on top of the endless body of water. The old-timers told stories about the seaports that have been, about bar fights, and tales of adventures about women lovers they had left behind. I couldn't say if those tales were real or imaginary.

I walked onto the deck, the ocean waves were gentle, and the sky streaked with various colors. Beyond the vast ocean, the setting sun illuminated the rolling waves folded gently against our ship. After listening to yet another an old-timer's story about a brawl he was involved in the Philippines, this was a welcoming site.

Before going to sleep that evening, I felt peaceful but soon I woke up from an abrupt jolting. I looked outside my porthole; under the pale moonlight, the gentle waves had swelled considerably and were crushing on the vessel. I sat on my bedside and reflected on the mysterious pounding that vibrated the earth when I was a child. I remembered the massive waves hitting the coastline with a tremendous force. Beyond my window, the trees bent under the whistling winds and the immense waves kept their rhythmical drumming. The sweeping winds, the gloomy sky, and the towering waves created a phenomenon that seemed paranormal. It was at once spectacular and yet terrified. I yearned for the outside, to go out and play. I wiped the foggy glass window to have a clear view beyond our yard. The majestic waves kept pounding, creating roars from the depth of the sea. Outside my window, two little birds were tucked on the corners of the window sill, trying to find safety from nature's destruction. I cracked the window open and let them in. Both of them crawled in the corner of the room and settled there feeling safe.

Sleep escaped me that night as the vessel's rhythmical swings intensified. By the morning hours, the hostile ocean waves were toying with our vessel. I walked out into the ship's hallway holding on the rail while the vessel tilted to a horizontal position. When the vessel descended to its side, I held my breath waiting for it to level. Instead, it swung and dropped to its other side. Most of the crew was sitting in the dining room area. Some of them were praying, others looking at pictures of loved ones or writing their last wishes, perhaps to stuff the notes into a bottle, seal it, and throw it into the sea. I have seen that in the movies, but I never thought I would live it. Whatever everyone was doing, there was a prevailing thought; survival was unlikely. This was it! This was the end!

The steel doors and porthole windows were tightly sealed to confine the crew in the living quarters. The blasts of the merciless ocean waves thrashing our defenseless ship along with the thunderous skies and the violent winds created a daunting atmosphere. I could only imagine what was happening outside. For some reason, the word cataclysm was stuck in my head. I associated cataclysmic events, like volcano eruptions, major earthquakes, or flooding rains, to some of the stories I heard growing up. I never thought I would be caught in one. My curiosity overpowered my fear and I walked up to the navigation bridge. The captain was the calmer of the three people in the bridge. The young Chief Officer seemed agitated while manning the navigation equipment and the quartermaster wrestled to control the steering wheel.

The scenery was surreal. The immense ocean waves were reaching for the dense clouds hanging low in the sky before confronting our ship head-on. The impact was of epic magnitude; each wave lifted the ship and kept it balanced, like a see-saw. The vessel hung on the top of the waves for a few heart-stopping moments. As the waves let the vessel down, bow first, it was swallowed by the ocean. Cracking noises echoed from the vessel's joints. What followed was an incredible emotional roller-coaster. The entire twenty-thousand-ton ship was buried in the ocean and uncertain if it would be able to emerge. When the dark clouds appeared beyond the bridge windows, my heart began to beat again. As the vessel surfaced, streams of foamy water surged from the ship's deck back into the ocean. It is peculiar that this particular scenery remains vivid in my mind. It was a feeling of survival amidst fascinating, untamed beauty. The momentary survival of the ship repeated over and again, as the waves kept lifting the vessel, before submerging it in the ocean once again.

"It doesn't look, good captain," I said in a somber voice. "Have faith my son, this vessel is an old timer and too tough to give in."

He was not convincing. He seemed tired. He had been awake for two days already, anticipating the cyclone, and there were several more days to go.

We stood defenseless at the mercy of nature's wrath. The waves kept coming determined to devour us. Every wave seemed like it was the last one to lift the vessel up and throw it back into the waters. I walked back down to the living quarters. Everyone was sitting silent with sober faces. No doubt they were thinking of their loved ones. I thought of my parents being devastated by the news. My parents were strong and had seen many tragedies, but this was different; to lose a child must be unimaginable suffering.

My mind reeled through precious memories; Kiato's soothing sunsets, my beloved Greek islands, my mother's backyard and my father's cooking. Beyond the ship's confined living quarters, the image of my calm blue sea erased the monster waves. The melancholic blackness of the sky above me turned into cherished blue sky dotted with myriads of stars.

But my imagination did not erase reality; the boundless waves kept the onslaught on the old ship. Grandmother, I love you, but you were wrong when you told me that I would live to be an old man and have children. There was no way that we could survive the wrath of the Pacific Ocean's waters. All communication with the outside world was disconnected; we were at the mercy of this natural phenomenon. I heard people talking about how destiny determines the course of life. But, what about the responsibility of our decisions? I thought of the comment my father frequently made during my vulnerable moments; "In life, you must make good choices because you can't escape the consequences of your decisions." I decided to get onto this ship headed for Japan. On every long and sleepless day on the weather-beaten ship, I did not condemn destiny or blamed God as many around me did; I had to live and die, with the decision I made.

The good news was that we survived another day and bad news was that we had another day of torture ahead of us. Everyone was tired and tense. Very few could close their eyes to get some sleep. I remember I tried to eat some soup and as the ship tilted one way, I had to lift the bowl the other way quickly taking a couple of swallows before switching hands and lifting the bowl the other way as the ship tilted to the other side. I don't know why that stuck in my mind. Maybe because it was the last fun thing I would have done.

It was that night, I guess, a little past midnight when I found myself sitting by my bedside, with my head buried in the palms of my hands trying desperately to keep awake. I did not want to die in my sleep. Suddenly everything went quiet. I opened my door: alarms were going off and people running down to the engine room.

"What happened?" I asked.

"The engines have stopped," someone said.

"You've got to be kidding me!"

I ran down to the engine room with the others to see if I could be of any help. The chief engineer and the entire engine crew were there, trying to identify the problem.

"It's the water pump. The engine is overheated, and it shut down." Someone said.

Hours went by as we worked frantically to correct the problem. It was impossible to stand still while the ship, without the power of the engine, was swinging widely. The floor steel panels of the engine room were filled with oil and we skidded all over the place. Someone brought ropes, we tied them around our waists then secured the other end into a pole to be able to stay in one spot.

It was about six hours before we got the engine running again. The good news was that the engine had stopped as the immense waves had subsided; we were in the aftermath of the cyclone. If this had happened a day or two before, we would have already been at the bottom of the sea.

By the next morning, the ship was floating on gentle rhythm swings and we were able to open the doors and the porthole windows. The daylight blinded my eyes and when I was able to see, there was the bright sky and a calm sea; sights which only yesterday I thought I would never see again. The deck of the ship was ravaged, but we had survived.

A few days later when we pulled into the port of Osaka, we learned that a Norwegian vessel had sunk during the same cyclone and not too far from our ship.

I looked proudly as the wrecked vessel ducked in the shipping yard for repairs. "You did great," I whispered. It was while I was in Osaka that I received a telegram saying that grandmother had passed. Just as she had told me. I would never see her again. I thought of her and the little chapel. After all, I could grow to be old and maybe someday I would have children.

I was glad that I escaped death but most important I survived to restore the faith in my grandmother.

Grandmother, I am sorry I doubted you.

Actual picture taken during the cyclone.

Shortly after surviving the immense ocean wave

13

FRIENDSHIP

The month of May was named to honor the Greek goddess Maia; goddess of spring. Maia, the eldest daughter of Atlas and mother of Hermes, is known for radiating her gentle fragrances and promoting the growth of flowers. It is not by chance that Maia is the most beautiful of her seven nymph sisters, all of whom we can see in the night skies in the Pleiades constellation. In Greece, the first day of May is a national holiday. During this month, there is no escaping the flower perfume and the omnipresent vibrant hues of wildflowers. The month when the earth is best decorated I believe to be the most inspiriting of months. By now the green blades piercing the earth in April have blossomed into sage, fennel, violets, daisies, poppies and other wildflowers. In the planes, the greenery of blooming olives, figs, and grapevines, along with the pomegranates, mulberries, and almond trees add to the canvas of breathless wild colors. On the mountains, the eucalyptus, thyme, oregano, pine and cypress trees complete another element to the Corinthian land that is blessed with bearing soil. Another thing that I loved is that the month of May proclaimed the end of our school year.

The summertime was a pleasant time in my hometown. The streets of the agora and our beach were crowded as more tourists flocked the city and natives returned to vacation with their families. I've always looked forward to the long lazy days of summer; a time when parents were more tolerant; there were no concerns about homework and grades.

The tension of schooling was replaced with perpetual summertime daydreams.

There was more time for soccer and visits to our movie theater were more frequent. Usually, the customary black-and-white brief newscasts before the movies were boring to a child anxious to see the movie. However, in one of those newscasts, I saw hunters killing elephants and other animals. I remember being traumatized by the cruelness of men. For several nights in my sleep, there were green forests, colorful birds, roaring lions, leaping monkeys, and disturbing images of dead elephant's babies. I spoke to my two best friends about my disturbing dreams and, being the great friends they were, they decided to help me.

In the summer of fifty-three, along with my two best friends, we planned our most ambitious journey. We wanted to travel to Africa, explore the vast forests and save the animals. Of course, for the three eight-year-old kids it was an imaginary adventure, but never-the-less we had to be prepared. The fundamental concern in this adventure was to be physically fit. Near our home was a wooded area and we made it into our training grounds. We exercised by climbing on trees, swinging on ropes and hanging from tree branches. In our young minds, there was no doubt we would get to Africa without any difficulty. We planned to ride in the back of a truck until we found a seaport, then sneak onto a ship that would take us to Africa.

When the day to execute our plan arrived, we made the

first steps towards our long journey. It was early afternoon and a good time to walk away from our town since everyone was taking a nap. The streets were empty, only periodically someone would pass by and looked at us with suspicion – that is what I thought anyway. All three of us acted cool and tried to hide our nervousness. We reached the small bridge on the outskirts of town and decided to sit on the side of the bridge and look for trucks and maybe a driver who would take pity on us and help with our big plan.

After a while, we broke our silence and proclaimed the end of this adventure.

"I'm hungry, what about you guys?" I said, turning to my friends. They looked at each other, then back at me and we all started to smile.

"Yeah, we both are pretty hungry," they said in one voice. As we headed back home, I thought of how much I would have missed my family if I had taken that imaginary journey. The three of us felt as if we were returning from a triumphant adventure. That is until I had to face my mother.

"Where have you been all afternoon? You missed your nap; I've been looking all over for you," she was not happy.

As usual, I said nothing and ran inside the house to escape her wrath. When I went to the taverna, later on, the enticing aroma of the food coming from my father's kitchen was the most exciting feeling on earth. My father was standing in the kitchen, preparing for dinner. I walked toward him and hugged him. He held me with love and I felt secure in his arms. For now, I thought, I would let my parents be my security. I would let them guard me against the dangerous people.

"I love you, dad," I said looking at him. His face lightens up with joy.

The food that day tasted better than ever. My mother had made taramosalata. She always made extra for me because she knew how much I love it and my father had made stefado for the customers. But he let me have some because he knew it was one of my favorite foods. As I was eating, I smiled thinking that there are no parents like mine anywhere in this universe, and if I were going, I would have missed the great pleasure of sitting for dinner with my family.

I often think about that imaginary adventure. It reminds me that it is okay to dream, to escape from reality, to alleviate our arrogance and to see the world through the child's eyes. I genuinely believe that, in merging the matured mind with the innocence of a child, we initiate unbiased opinions.

Throughout my life, I used that single event to characterize a friendship; when someone is willing to walk to the end of this earth to help you as my two little friends did. This, my friends, is the definition of friendship.

14

DEFIANCE

It was a hot summer day; the asphalt on the road was soft, the trees were dehydrated, and the vegetation wilted. Thankfully for the earth, the summer was near the end, and autumn was coming to the rescue. As I was walking down the lonely road, my only companion was the unending cacophony from the multitudes of locusts.

I was about halfway to my destination after an hour and a half of walking. Suddenly there was a sign of life. A jeep with young tourists went by me, only to stop a few meters beyond. The four tourists, riding in the open-top car, with music blasting, were cheerful as they started talking to me. With my limited English, I understood that they were willing to give me a ride. "Come on, come on," they kept encouraging me over the sounds of "Twist and Shout." I smiled and waved, "Thanks, I am okay." The carefree youngsters made a gesture of a peace-sign and drove away.

I was nearly eighteen-years-old, just finished college and had my engineering degree. My dad suggested that I should join the Air Force, to continue my engineering education and at the same time fulfill my military obligation to my country. He thought it would be a good idea because the military structure would subdue my free-spirited mind. I wanted to tell him, "Dad, free-spirit is okay, and I am not sure if engineering is my calling in life. I want to be a soccer player." But disappointing my dad was out of the question. So, I went.

Since joining the Air Force was voluntary, I had the option to opt-out anytime during

basic training. I thought our trainers were cruel, treating us as if we were brainless and worthless. So, I left. There was no transportation available from that remote Air Force base in northeast Peloponnese and so I decided to walk to the nearest town, about three hours by foot.

I remember that hot summer day walking on the winding road, wondering if I had done the right thing – if walking away from a situation I did not like was just the easy way out.

I perceived that long road ahead of me was my path to my freedom. I did not think for a moment that walking away from the military base was my fault. In fact, for a fleeting moment, I blamed my father. He was the one, after all, who taught me that my freedom was my most precious possession. The heat was unbearable.

I sat under a tree to rest and to gather my thoughts. Ahead of me was uncertainty and behind me a road of no return. I think about that walk often and paraphrase it with life; An endless path which at the end seems that it was just a few miles long.

Back then I paid little attention to the virtues of life. I've always had this silent desire to read more and to write my thoughts; to observe life and give it back in the form of ideas. I wanted to see things that others don't see, feel things that others don't feel, to imagine things that others neither imagine nor anticipate. To find water in the desert, food in any land, hope in any despair, and peace in every war; to move the world and change it.

After some rest, I went on. By the time I was at the end of the road, my legs were exhausted, my back hurt, and my mind confused.

When I reached the town of my destination, I was dizzy from the heat and I was thirsty. Entering the small town and finding life waiting beyond the loneliness of the road was a welcome sight. It was late afternoon. I found myself among strangers who looked at me with curious glances. I was a stranger among them after all. I found the bus station and took the bus going to my hometown.

I remember riding on the bus; I tried to imagine my father's face when entering the taverna. I wasn't sure about his reaction.

Darkness had fallen when the bus finally arrived in Kiato. The tables outside the taverna were full of people. Meats were roasting on the charcoal rotisserie by the door and familiar scents of food overflowing the street.

I noticed the surprised look on my father's face when he saw me walking in the taverna. That was his only reaction. He then went on to do his work. He took the time to dish a plate of food for me and after the dinner rush we sat down to talk. He was calm. He spoke for a while and, as usual, I bowed my head and listened. His wisdom did not send me back to the road that I came from but prepared me for the challenging ways ahead.

Before walking in the taverna, I remember the silent pain inside of me. I felt an urge to discipline my behavior, avoiding future mistakes. But when I left my dad, I felt that mistakes are acceptable if they became lessons. He also told me that I was brave to do what I did. According to him, the definition of braveness is to be willing to follow your truth.

Now I am thinking, considering how many lessons I have learned in my life; there must have been countless mistakes.

15

REGRETS

When I was a young boy, it was my turn to climb on the tall bell tower and ring the large church bell. The deafening sound of the ringing bell resonated in my eardrums and throbbed in my head. I never had such a tormenting feeling again until the day, when I was laying on the top bed of the double-decker military bunk, blazing spikes were thrust inside my head and there was an extreme pounding on my brains. A torrent of needles launched from the light bulbs, piercing my eyes - it was like that bell; intense, debilitating.

There was sweat on my forehead and tears in my eyelids. If I could only fall in sleep to end this endless torment. The suffering pain from hell stopped hours later when the doctor's medication put me to sleep.

In the morning, I was in a bizarre paralyzed state. A transparent aura restrained my senses. It felt like I was floating in a zone where I was neither asleep nor awake. Suddenly I felt my blanket moving and then someone was pulling my leg. The diaphanous aura vanished to reveal my sergeant, throwing my blanket on the floor and pulling my leg. I closed my eyes, "please god-of-sleep, let me die again – for an hour or two." I begged. "Get up and sweep the room," his voice brought back the sound of the church bells, hurting my brains once again. I wanted to tell him, something that he already knew, that I was under doctor's orders to stay off duty for three days, but I doubted he would listen. I remained silent.

"Did you hear what I said?" That voice again – please stop. Following the angry voice, there was a violent pulling of my legs and arms trying to force me down. "What did I do to deserve this ridiculous person?"

Maybe I should have gotten down from my bed and swept the room, to entertain this fixation he seemed to always have with me. But before I could finish my thoughts, I found myself falling off my bed. Once down on my feet, he grabbed my left arm and pulled me toward him. Before I had a chance to use logic, I lifted my right fist and punched him in the face, then with the left and the right again. He lay across on the other row of beds. Blood poured from his nose. It happened fast, but as soon as it happened, I knew I should not have done it. This was totally out of character for me; I had always despised violence. Within seconds the room was full of other soldiers and soon the military police arrived.

"Arrest him," he screamed pathetically, pointing his finger at me. The military police escorted me to the commander's office. The commander lectured me for a while and told me that he would recommend a court-martial hearing for assaulting an officer.

Five months before this event, I proudly walked, along with eleven others, into the Army's Air Force Academy, an elite branch of the Greek military. We've been transferred from the town of Tripolis, where we did our sixty-day mandatory basic training, to be educated as Air Force engineers; eleven of us as aircraft specialists and myself as a helicopter specialist.

The military grounds in Pahni, a small village near the town of Megara, was more like a college campus than a military base. The small compound was overlooking the sea and beyond the plethora of trees, there was an endless sandy beach. After passing the small front gate, we waited by the guard-post for instructions. A sergeant-major wearing a stern look on his face strolled toward us. He stopped a few meters before us and quietly stared at each one of us as we announced our names. The sergeant, who was a medium height and probably in his late thirties, held his hands behind his waist and stood still. We waited for him to say something, but he kept looking at the ground and it seemed that he was in a deep trance of thoughts.

We looked at each other, wondering about this unusual approach of meeting the new cadets, and waited anxiously for him to come out of his trance. Finally, he lifted his head and began to look at us once again. He then approached each one of us; his sidesteps were swift and his eyes steadfast.

This humorous approach of introducing himself amused me; maybe it was his intimidation technique. Or maybe he has been watching too many military movies.

A few years earlier, when I had voluntarily enlisted to serve the Air Force, I developed a distasteful perspective about authorities who treated newly enlisted soldiers like brainless beings. All twelve of us just completed our basic training where military authorities were yelling in our faces calling us unkind names and treating us with contempt.

When the sergeant sidestepped in front of me, his face inches away from mine, staring into my eyes. I stared back. I stood in confusion; was this a silly game, like when we were children having a staring contest? Then he spoke for the first time.

"I don't know if I like you. You better behave if you want to get along with me," he said. I was surprised he had a voice. I wanted to smile and say, "but, I like myself just fine. How come you don't like me?" but I thought I better not. I knew that I was not going to say what he wanted to hear - "Yes sir, sergeant." I smiled and that seemed to infuriate him.

During my training, I learned that he was a trained helicopter engineer. Perhaps the reason that I was the only one from the group to studying to be one was threatening to him. I will never know. This is one of those defining moments, one that, when I look back, I wonder what life would have been if I had never met this person. I had every intention to add to my college engineering studies and broaden my knowledge of aeronautical engineering. I could have made an excellent living working in this fast-developing field.

On that day, when I entered the gate of the Army's Air Force base, I was perfectly content with the idea of entering a space to gain knowledge, to enrich my mind. However, I wasn't going to do it by kneeling in front of a madman. I did not think that it should be like basic training where some sergeant-tyrant screams at your ear and ask you to do push-ups and crawl up to the hill on your knees.

In this military camp, there were about sixty people and it seemed that the sergeant singled me out and reported me for every little error and insisted that I be punished. Punishment in the Greek military is done by imposing jail time. You do not exactly go to jail, but the time of your punishment is added to your two years of mandatory service.

I had always prided myself in the fact that I could get along with anyone, no matter their origin or ideology. My parents taught never to discriminate but never tolerate disrespect; this was rooted deep in my conscience.

The final blow with my sergeant happened about one month before my training was to be completed. For the last five months, I had been trying to compose myself, even though my sergeant reported me for every minor incident and piled up my "jail time." The classes were challenging at first but became easier as I began to comprehend the aerodynamic fundamentals of the helicopter mechanism and the theory and applications of flying operations.

The more I learned about helicopters; the more I developed a restrained admiration for the sergeant - he had to be a smart person to graduate these difficult classes. Unfortunately, his social skills disguised his intelligence. I was looking forward to completing my training and being transferred to another post until my illness clouded my judgment. I was determined not to miss any classes. I was able to handle the high fever and the watery eyes. But when the familiar sound of the church bell detonated in my eardrums and throbbed my brains, I decided to go to the doctor. He gave me medication and three days duty-free, to stay in bed. "Stay in bed. You can always catch up with your classes," The doctor said.

After the unfortunate event, I was to be under surveillance and not allowed to leave the camp and I was dismissed from classes and any other activity. I was more disappointed with myself than anything else.

As soon as my father heard of the incident, he went to work to solve the problem. He was not angry with me, but he was not supportive of my action either. I believe he thought that what was done was not going to change. Avoiding further consequences was more important.

I appeared in front of the court-martial judges almost thirty days after the incident. In the meantime, my father and mother had worked hard to make the necessary connections that would help them give me a more lenient punishment. My father made many trips to Athens, and my mother spent endless hours in the military court waiting to talk to various officers about my character. Because of them, I knew my sentence even before I appeared in front of the panel. My punishment was the dismissal from the Army Air Force. I was to be transferred to the town of Serres in northern Greece, to finish my remaining military time as a utility soldier. The future now was uncertain and my attitude about life was problematic at best. I was disobedient and careless.

Then one-morning pandemonium happened; there were bright lights, bugle calls, officers running in the leaving quarters, loud voices urging soldiers to get up, to move faster. Soon after I was listening to passionate speeches about patriotism; reciting the usual nationalistic triplet to provoke emotions; Duty, God, and Country.

The day was April 21, 1967, a day every Greek remembers. That day, a single event changed the course of my life.

16

THE DREAM

The night before that fateful day of April stood in absolute silence. My mind was restless with reflections of the past and ideas about the future.

A light bulb on a pole was casting its meager light into the room through the misty window. I imagined the frost ahead in the early morning and I wrapped myself tighter in my blanket. Even though it was springtime, the winter frostiness had carried over this year.

Other than occasional snoring, someone tossing around, or a squeaky bedspring, there was quietness in our room that housed twenty-four of us, sleeping in double bunks.

I thought of the morning ahead, the daily routine; the bugle call to wake us up, a sound of annoyance. There will be sleepy voices, soldiers muttering words of displeasure for interrupting their sleep. The lights will go on, and some will pull their blankets up to cover their eyes to avoid that awful glare. "Oh, God, is it morning already?" some will murmur. "Come on, turn those lights off," others will whisper.

After the rising call, we would have just a few minutes to wash our faces, shave, make our beds impeccably, shine our boots, make sure that our uniforms were immaculate, and then a quick breakfast before lining up for body count and on to our daily assignments.

The life on my new military base was routinely and I, like everyone else, counted the days, the months, to be dismissed and get on with my civilian life.

Two years of our lives were given to serve our country. At first, it felt like a burden. As young men, we wanted to go to the beach with our friends, to lazily sit at the outdoor cafés in the evening, go to a movie, or a club at night. We missed the excitement of the soccer matches on Sundays. We yearned for the comfort of our bed and home cooking.

However, after our military duty was over, we went back to our neighborhoods as different thinking people, ready to reason with responsibilities.

The post-military era was a step towards maturity, a sense of patriotism and unwavering love for a country that we revered.

My thoughts faded away as I felt my eyelids weaken and soon my senses surrendered to a much-needed sleep. But, after a few minutes, I was up and running again.

I was running in a field of brown grapevines, bare of grapes. The branches of the vine resembled long dark needles. The ground was black, reminding me of the aftermath of a fire.

Thick drops of sweat were dripping from my forehead. I ran like a deer into the woods, soaked in sweat. Beyond the vineyards, there were orchards of leafless olive, almond, and citrus trees; their fruit discarded on the ground, deserted and decayed. The tree branches swerved like snakes reaching out to get me so, the faster I ran. The land was black, and I was barefooted. I scouted the grounds for a piece of soil untouched by the fire, to stop running, to rest.

I glanced behind me; people were chasing me, closing in on me. I couldn't see anybody; I only heard their footsteps growing closer. I tried to run faster, but the faster I went, the sound of the footsteps became louder. I could not understand how that was possible; I was strong, full of life, leaping like a tiger.

Soon after loud voices were hurting my ears; like thousands of bees swirling inside my head. I ran into a cluster of hills; nothing reminded me of the green hills I knew. These hills were like enormous stones loaded one on top of another, dark and barren. A feeling of relief overcame me; at least I could hide and rest there for a while. I ran toward the rocks, my feet bleeding, my heart beating fast.

Suddenly a man appeared on the top of one of the stone hills. He was wearing a uniform, full of decorations. This stern-faced man was waving to the invisible people chasing me,

"Go, faster, get him," demanded with a resounding voice.

From the darkened skies an enormous vulture descended from the thick clouds. It was circling above the decorated man, planning its attack. I was certain that the vulture was about to fall upon my head.

Suddenly, this enormous beast swerved in descent and grasped the extended arm of the man in the decorated uniform. When the vulture's legs touched the man's arm, a great fire erupted beyond the hills; a great rumble shook the earth. I ran along the arid, desolated land for safety. A great sadness overpowered my heart as I saw my beautiful land burned and with vast ruptures opening everywhere. The great fire in the sky became a rolling thunder, an awful noise, and then creepy darkness infused fear onto every living creature.

Suddenly, amidst the destruction, the sun appeared in the far east, only it was not the bright sun I knew, it was like a tray with burning candles blowing in the wind. The air began to seethe, the earth whirled, and I whirled with it, faster and faster it turned.

Dizziness overcame me. Sweat ran over my entire body. The sheets on my bed were soaked from it. The sound of the military bugle call was real this time.

I looked out of the window expecting to see the meager rays of the sun laboring up from the east, but there was darkness. I closed my eyes, trying to avoid that annoying light bulb on the outside poll. Only, a few moments later the lights multiplied and our room, along with the entire military compound, was lit up.

Murmurs of sleepy voices filled the room. Some of the soldiers jumped out of their bunks while others turned over, seeking a few more moments under the warm covers. The bugler blew his horn, this time with force as if he was annoyed with the ones still in bed.

I slowly lifted myself up and sat on the edge of my bed. I buried my head in the palms of my hands, pressing the sides of my skull. I wanted to squeeze that dream out of my brain, but it stayed there – stubborn, vivid, annoying.

The sweat of my body forced chills through my spine. I wrapped my blanket around
me. I could not tell if it was the morning frost or the dream that made my body shiver. I missed the sun's warmth; I wondered why it was not up yet. There was something wrong; this was not a standard time for the wake-up call.

I sat on the side of my bed trying to convince myself that this was an error and soon the lights would go off and I would be under the warm covers once more.

But, the bugle sounded again, this time calling us to assemble, it seemed determined and commanding, cutting into the darkness like a whistling whip, daring us to stay still.

No time to wash our faces or to shave. To a Greek, not washing his face in the morning is a bad omen. Soldiers rushed to make their beds, unhappy with this early call.

What was this all about?

I remembered my dream and wondered if something dreadful was about to happen.

"Oh, this is stupid," I thought. "I don't believe in dreams. Superstitious people try to make sense out of a nonsensical dream." Analyzing the future with dreams, coffee grounds, or palm and card readings, was indeed a different belief for me.

Our sergeant, a bulldog of a man, ran into our barracks barking out orders. He was nervous like a man trusted with a secret and not knowing how to act without revealing it.

"You too. You too! What is the matter with you, didn't you hear the call?" He was looking at me, moving his arms, and pointing to the door.

I got dressed and hurried outside. The great uproar had awakened at least my curiosity.

"This is probably a drill, an exercise," I thought.

"What is happening, sergeant?" soldiers were asking as they were moving towards outside.

"Move on, move on, no questions." The sergeant growled, looking very serious.

As the dawn of the day appeared in the distant grim sky, I heard a thunderous sound and looked up to see a swarm of military planes flying south. The movement of heavy military machinery sounded from the opposite side of our base.

The emergency sirens shrilled, calling us for a swift

gathering. Soldiers fanned out, running to assemble in the front yard, panicking at the thought that it might be a call to war.

When everyone had assembled, the hierarchy of our base was present, standing on a stage in front of the troops. The unusual presence of our base commander made everyone run faster than usual; he was a tyrant of a man. His cold, dark eyes sent fear through the most fearless minds. He walked as if he was a piece of steel; unemotional.

"This is serious." I thought as everyone around me was running, carrying their weapons, confused and anxious.

Our commander's voice carried across the yard, quieting everyone. All soldiers stood breathless, anticipating his orders. The morning air, freezing and merciless, made our bodies tremble, but no one dared to move. It was so quiet, so surreal, that I could hear the sound of the gentle wind whistling in the top of the trees.

"Today, we must save our country," he began with his speech. He talked about enemies to the sovereignty of the country and dark forces that had corrupted our youth. He spoke of social enemies, corrupt political administrations. Words that sounded familiar, coming out of the mouth of a dictator.

"The military is taking over the business of our country to save our nation for a better tomorrow for our children."

A thunderbolt struck inside my heart as I realized that he just announced a military coup.

He continued, "All must take your weapons. You will be assigned to different locations. No civilian will be able to walk in the streets until advance orders. You must order every citizen to go home or be arrested."

The realization that the military has taken over the business of the country was terrifying.

As the commander continued to emphasize the danger for Greece from enemy forces. I wondered who this enemy was. My thoughts were interrupted by a few soldiers walking in front of the commander throwing their weapons on the ground on a protest to the dictators.

The stars and the coronas on the olive-green uniforms became irrelevant. The thought of arresting peaceful citizens, forcing them into their homes nauseate me. An unknown force surfaced from the depths of my heart and commanded my right leg to move, then the left, and guided me to the front of the line.

My eyes crossed paths with the commander's eyes. "I am not afraid of you," I whispered. My choice was clear; I tossed my rifle on the pile of the other weapons.

The commander and the rest of the brass were visually infuriated. "You know what we call your disobedience? Treason. You have no idea about the consequence of your actions," the commander shouted - his face red with anger.

I glanced at the few soldiers who took this stand; they seemed calm and unmoved by the threats. I relaxed; I was okay with the consequences. The commander unaccustomed to disobedience, became hostile, his eyes brimmed with venom as he looked at us and then at his officers beckoning his orders to arrest the rebelling soldiers.

Three sergeants stepped towards us, lifted their rifles bringing them down with force, hitting the rebelling soldiers with the rifle butts. Some were hit on the stomach, others behind the head. I doubled over from the forceful hit on my stomach. Then some of the other officers along with a few soldiers stood behind us and pushed us forward, escorting us to the detention center.

I saw faces of people who yesterday I called friends, suddenly pointing their guns at me. Boys with whom I played soccer with, who sat next to me at the dining table, lads who yesterday, joked, shared and bonded through our military duty of serving our country. Now they are pointing guns at their friends.

I watched their puzzled faces. One of them had tears dripping from his eyes. Those who believed the military propaganda wore stern faces, while others were looking at us with a begging expression, as if they were thinking, "Please don't make us do this."

The face of the person walking next to me was cut and bleeding. I reached into my pocket to pull out my handkerchief, but a shove shook my back. "Don't move," a voice whispered in my ear.

I looked back at him and said, "what is the matter with you?" He looked away.

Once in the detention center, we knew that in the military anyway, we were already labeled with ideological epithets. The dictators will spread forth epithets like socialists, liberals, or radicals to justify their actions. We were none of that; we were youngsters standing up against aggression and human decency – too young to be concerned about left and right, red or blue.

Greeks defend their political affiliations with passion. Usually, a Greek is identified by three epithets: The family name, the name of the soccer team they support, and their affiliated political name, such as "leftist, nationalist, centrist, socialist, communist, fascist," and so on.

Generally, Greeks believe passionately in democracy and individual freedom. There are common arguments in the streets, the cafés, and everywhere else there is a gathering. This morning of April, something new had happened to shatter the structure of our generation, and to ignite new argument but, this one situation was enforcing the law of oppression; a law against democratic principles.

Now that the military dictators had overthrown its civilian government, poverty, hunger, economic and social issues had become secondary. Now, everyone had to honor and obey the new masters. For some of us, the love for our homeland did not allow us to welcome these new rulers. As we were locked up in the detention center, one of the officers proclaimed, "You'll be sorry you were born." Not sure what he meant by that but I for one I was proud to be born in this land. In the next few days following this event, there were thousands of citizens arrested for no reason other than their political affiliations. The detention centers, jails and even big halls and soccer stadiums were overflowing with prisoners. It was a time that democracy was abused. The peculiar thing for me was that some people accepted the injustice and sided with the offenders.

To believe in freedom of expression and tolerate any oppression is nothing short of an oxymoron.

My Heroes, My Town

17

CONVICTIONS

The Sunday sky above Attica was draped with its familiar deep blue color. The bright morning sun had just departed from the far horizon and was on its way for the long journey to the other side of that magnificent sky. In the suburbs of Athens, people emerged on the narrow streets strolling towards the squares and the outdoor cafes. The Greek flags stood motionless on the balconies. Mouthwatering aromas spilled out into the streets as homemakers had begun to prepare food and sweets. Large groups of people gathered in the outdoor cafes to plan their day over frappé. The usual subjects of politics, football, philosophy and leisure were put aside this Sunday morning. The major subject was the "big event." Most of the people were standing arguing loudly and with dramatic gestures about the event that was going to take place later in the day in downtown Athens.

Royalists and conservatives engage in vigorous dialogues with the liberals and the centrists. As usual, the battle of words and gestures changed no one's position on their beliefs.

The arguments ended because it was time to go. Soon everyone abandoned the cafes and blended into the massive traffic jam of cars and motorbikes, heading towards the center of Athens. Long lines of people stood at the bus stations and the metro platforms, waiting for a ride to witness the "big event."

The streets, the balconies and the rooftops from Syntagma Square to Omonia Square and on to the Orthodox Cathedral were brimming with people trying to find a spot on the sidewalk, seeking the perfect view. Scores of police officers and men of the armed forces formed a human chain along the sidewalks. The sun was now midway of its journey. The sky had become a flaming wheel casting its merciless rays on the crowded bodies of the Athenians.

I was nineteen years old on that day, the 18th of September of 1964. I was at an age when a bubble was growing inside of me, a bubble full of inexplicable subjects. Since birth, I've been a part of a society that surrounded me with complexity and aspiration. Behind the walls of simplistic lifestyles was a labyrinth full of wisdom, contradictory beliefs and firm convictions. Those subjects were seeded in the freshly plowed surface of my heart and now, at my young age, the blades of enchanting flowers and poisonous weeds began to surface rapidly, side by side. It was an age in which beliefs and convictions were about to burst, insolent and free, to become opinions and lifestyles.

I found myself wandering on Stadiou Street by the Omonia Square, surrounded by people, young and old, dressed in their Sunday clothes, some of them were holding flowers, others waving flags. Everyone was anxious for a glance at the royalty. "They are coming…they are coming," people shouted, and the excitement intensified. Sounds of hands clapping and gasps of admiration sounded on my left, from where the parade was approaching. Everyone stretched their necks in that direction, the hands of the people were extended to the street, offering flowers, waving the blue and white flags. The armed forces struggled to keep the anxious crowd on the sidewalks. Flowers and confetti rained from the rooftops and the balconies. People screamed in my ears and stepped on my feet; I knew then that the showcase of the parade was near where I was standing. I stretched my neck to see.

A team of men from the military police was leading the pack, riding on motorcycles. Behind them, elite men of the cavalry were riding beautiful chestnut horses. The flowers kept falling from above to create a flower bed on the hot asphalt. Soon I saw the spectacle. Gorgeous white horses were pulling a black carriage decorated with golden emblems and rolling on red wheels.

The newlyweds were riding in the carriage. They were very young; he was handsome, and she was beautiful. He wore his white royal uniform, decorated with emblems and she was in a glamorous, long, white dress. They smiled and waved to the crowd, the crowd that they would rule someday. He was Konstantinos, the crown prince of Greece and she was princess Anna Maria of Denmark. The horses pulled the carriage toward the royal palace, by the Syntagma Square. The clapping and the shouting of the people followed the carriage's route. Behind the royal couple, a platoon of chestnut horses paraded in synchronized steps.

A long line of expensive, convertible cars, loaded with royalty and heads of state from around the world, followed the parade. The guests of honor waved to the crowd, but the spectators had lost interest and began to move away from the sidewalks.

I turned and walked away from the crowd, not because I had lost interest, but because an uneasy feeling was settling in my stomach. I could not look at that street any longer; there was confusion in my head, as mixed thoughts began to surface. At first, I did not know how to classify the event I just witnessed.

Was it a comedy or a celebration?

I sat on a bench to collect my thoughts. Thousands of people fanned out through the streets of Athens; thousands more walked down to the metro station. I observed their faces as they walked by. I saw expressions of admiration, disbelief, disappointment and relief. It was like the crowd that comes out from the theater, uncertain about the meaning of the play. The streets were now empty.

Sweepers began to pick up the confetti and the flowers, preparing the city for the nightlife. The hot sun was reaching the western horizon, leaving behind the melodramatics. I closed my eyes. Behind my eyelids appeared another crowd; the people in this crowd were in a different mood. They had expressions of sadness on their faces and tears in their eyes. Those were the faces that I observed ten months earlier, when, ironically, I was standing in the same area.

It was the 22nd of November 1963, when I too let uncontrollable tears pour from my eyes. It was the day that the world lost another hope, a day of great loss and deep mourning. Loss and mourning are two sentiments, when united, create unbearable pain, the kind of pain that can crystallize injustice and hope into a paragon of truth.

The death of John Kennedy changed the course of history and possibly the direction of the United States of America and how the world defined their relationship to this superpower.

For me, it was those two events, a flawless comedy, and a somber tragedy, that truly shaped my beliefs. It was only then that I remember the overburdened bubble finally burst inside of me. It has been a long time since I've begun to wonder about fate and how the outcome of history can be affected by various events.

Is fate accidental, or is it conclusive?

In my long and peripatetic life, I have tried to analyze philosophical propositions. Nothing has puzzled me more than the issue of fate.

Sitting on the bench that September day, I thought about the crown prince of Greece and John Kennedy. One was born with the privilege to rule a nation because of his bloodline, even though not one citizen voted for him - this to my knowledge is the antithesis of democracy.

The other earned the people's trust, inspired an entire generation and fought tirelessly for democratic principle and social justice. His death silenced the voice of hope.

We think about historical events and how they alter the course of history. The assassinations of Abraham Lincoln, John and Bobby Kennedy, Martin Luther King, Mahatma Gandhi, are events that shifted the focus of the world and touched an entire generation for the better.

A knot crept into my stomach. A similar knot was stuck in my throat ten months ago when bullets of hate silenced the hero of countless people.

I stood up and looked around me. Dusk had covered the eternal city. The streets behind me were bare of flowers and confetti. The applause and the roar had become a soundless echo. At the age of nineteen, I began my quest for my identity. It was a time that I began to identify the blades surfacing in my heart and I began to separate them.

On one side were the blades that hurt, those that frighten and rule with malignity.

On the other side were the gentle blades that projected a certain beauty of sensitivity and calmness.

It was then, at a tender age, that I decided to become part of the brigade of those who care, those who oppose, those who carry an olive branch; the ones who do not bow to power, applaud the charade, or throw away beautiful flowers on the hot asphalt. The crisp breeze of Attica caressed my face. Ahead of me towered the sacred hill of the Acropolis. On the top of the hill, colorful lights projected the majestic image of the Parthenon, a symbol of human triumph.

I walked away convinced that, for me, those two events had contributed to a monumental personal triumph.

Defining times

18

DEATH OF A WARRIOR

Christmas is a day of ambivalence for me; a time of birth and a time of death. Thirty-four years after the Christmas morning of 1945, the day I was born, my father was killed. And so, the coexistence of two conflicting emotions began to infiltrate into my psyche and have been forcing my feelings towards two opposite directions ever since.

Just before the confrontation of joy and sorrow, I was driving from Los Angeles to Phoenix, anxious to join my family for Christmas.

The day before Christmas was full of joy. There was shopping and playing with my children and, as we were getting ready to open gifts, the phone rang.

It was after the telephone call that I felt an abrupt emotion. I felt the walls of my head swelling and my chest tightening. I remember that pain clearly, it was excruciating.

I walked outside of the house to breathe the fresh air. I sat on a bench, trying to grasp reality. Even the bright yellow moon on the ominous sky was an anomaly.

Images of my father's sometimes stern, other times radiant, but now a motionless face and my mother's always luminous but now a saddened expression dashed through my mind.

Strangely, sitting under the moonlight, I thought about love. The principle of love, for me anyway, was an ongoing theoretical argument that always puzzled me because of its multiple definitions. At that night though, I felt that the trueness of love was unpretentious and infinite. The love from my parents has already given me much more beyond my expectations. It inspired me to pursue my dreams. It taught me that the endless oceans were nothing but little lakes, and the mountaintops were just sand-piles on the beach. It inspired me to walk against the wind and dream in the rain.

I cried that night. All my inner strength was unable to stop the tears.

One of my heroes had fallen victim to a careless driver who left him alone to die in the dark, rainy night before Christmas.

I tried to picture my father, alone, dying on a cold sidewalk of Leoforos Sygrou in Athens, and I tried to imagine his last moments of life. I wondered how much he suffered, and the only comforting thought was that there was no pain.

I managed to get airline tickets to fly from Los Angeles to Athens. As I was driving back to Los Angeles, the highway seemed endless and the surroundings wrapped in darkness. The highway was empty, besides being Christmas eve, it was the great gasoline shortage.

The global supply of crude oil declined notably in the aftermath of the Iranian Revolution that ended in early 1979 with the fall of the monarch of Iran Shah Mohammad Reza Pahlavi.

Amidst massive protests, the Shah Pahlavi fled the country and Ayatollah Khomeini became the new leader of Iran. During the unrest, the Iranian oil exports were suspended, throwing world oil markets into disarray and generating intense distress among oil-importing countries.

During the day, all over the United States, long lines of cars, some stretched a few city blocks, were formed outside every open gas station. Often, after the long wait, drivers would find signs like, "Pumps closed" or "No gas."

As I drove on the lonely freeway towards Los Angeles, I imagined a faraway place thirty-four years ago when my mother was ready to give birth to her third child. Grandmother had told me that it was a cold night. All our family sat around the fireplace waiting. My mother lay in the next room, my father held her hand and my grandmother helped her to give birth. The room was lighted only with a couple of burning oil lamps. It was past midnight when my mother brought me into this world. My grandmother said that mother's face was overwhelmed with a pride, and father wrapped me in his arms and could not stop looking at me.

Now, ironically, thirty-four years from my birth to his death, I was rushing back to the same town where I was born to see him one last time before he was put to rest.

The highway in the desert seemed endless. At some point, I began to worry because my car was very low on gas. From the time I left the house in Phoenix, I had searched for an open gas station, but the gasoline crisis forced serving stations to close at nights.

As I approached Los Angeles in the early morning hours, I recounted the story my youngest brother told me. That night before Christmas father walked to the store to buy some groceries to prepare Christmas dinner for the family.

My father loved to cook. Now retired from the taverna he insisted on cooking for his family and friends. On his way back home, walking on the sidewalk, he was hit by a car. He was found sometime past midnight, dead. When the police called our home in Athens with the news, no one could believe it. Everyone thought it was a mistaken identity. My two older brothers went to the morgue to identify him. The guard refused to let them in because it was late at night, but my brothers were determined to know.

One of my brothers walked to the back of the building. He broke a window and entered the morgue to search for father's body. The guard heard the noise and went in to check what was wrong. My other brother warned him not to interfere. The guard, moved by this action, guided my brothers to my father. The brothers lifted my father's body, stood him up on his feet and with tears in their eyes asked him to walk. "Come on, Father. Men like you don't die. Come on. Walk."

But he would never physically walk again.

The weather of California matched my eyes. The rain was pouring from the dark skies. As I approached Anaheim, the car ran out of gas. I ran in the torrential rains to look for a telephone. I called a friend, and she came to pick me up and drove me to the Los Angeles International Airport. The delay of running out of gas made me miss my flight. The airline boarded me on another plane, to go through New York and Rome.

As I sat in the airport on Christmas Day waiting for my flight, I looked at the thousands of people moving in and out of the airport. Every one of them had a different story to tell about their experiences, their pains, and joys. I saw strange faces but sensed universal emotions. I wondered if they knew my anxiety or if they cared.

I do not remember the flight very well. My thoughts were

with my family.

I felt my father's arms around me, like that tender moment in the taverna when I was a little boy – more tears.

I remember when we were young and we asked our father for money to go to the movies. He would take the money and enclose it in his fist then tell us if we could open it the money would be ours. It was always impossible as if his hand was made of iron. All of us tried together and sometimes we succeeded only when he let us win.

In my teenage years, I often got into trouble. My father very seldom became excited or upset. He would sit across from me and talk. The conversation would be about life and virtues and would go on for a while. I always lowered my head and listened without even looking at him, as if I wanted to avoid the eyes that still paralyzed my senses. I listened to his words of wisdom about responsibilities and the virtues of life. He talked about our behavior and how it could affect others; to never be selfish, nor greedy, he said.

When I was very young, it was not possible to comprehend his way of thinking, but as I grew older, I began to understand his wisdom.

The resting place of my parents

19

LOST AND FOUND

The plane landed at the Athens Airport as the sun was setting on the western horizon. I was anxious to drive to Kiato and see my father for the last time.

I called my sister-in-law who was waiting for me in my parent's home in Athens, to drive with me to Kiato.

"We are too late," she said. "They have to bury him before the sunset."

Suddenly, I felt useless. I couldn't even make my father's funeral in time.

The orthodox church forbids embalming because you are not to tamper with the body. The wake of the deceased person is held the night following death, and the burial takes place the next day before sunset.

Waiting for a taxi cab, I looked at the sun; I wish I could slow down its course. I asked the taxi driver if it was possible to take me to Kiato before dark. "At any cost," I begged.

"There is no way," he said, shaking his head.

I asked him to take me home. Driving through the streets of Athens, I only noticed a few things different. So many years had gone by. I was drifting apart from the people I loved, and I was becoming a stranger to the country I admired.

As the taxicab stopped in front of my parent's home, the thought that I was not going to see my father one last time devastated me. I tried to imagine his funeral and the streets they carried him through. Those were the same streets he had stepped on so many times. I was sure there were hundreds of people attending his funeral.

My sister-in-law greeted me on the stairs. She couldn't stop her tears. I walked into my parents' bedroom. Pictures of their children sat on top of the furniture, my father's clothes hung neatly in the closet, and his black shoes were laying shiny underneath them.

That simple room brought back so many memories.

I walked around the small house as if I wanted to absorb every memory of him while his presence was fresh. I heard noises from downstairs. I looked down and saw my mother, brothers, and sister and a few other people coming up to the second-floor apartment where my parents lived. My mother was climbing the stairs slowly and with great difficulty. She seemed tired and when she finally got up the marble stairs, I saw her remarkable courage still painted on her face.

I held her, and endless love sprang out of my heart. She held me like never before; she didn't want to let me go. "Thank you, God," she whispered, "I lost my husband, but you brought back my son."

What I had just heard was extraordinary. She had just buried the love of her life, but my presence brought her joy. I felt guilty as I realized how selfish I had been. The years of my travels were too many. The time away from them was too long.

That day I discovered emotions I never knew existed. I spent most of the night talking to my mother, reminiscing the events of yesteryears. I felt closer to her than ever before.

The next morning I drove to Kiato with my mother and sister. My mother told me there were hundreds of people at the funeral. My three brothers and one of my cousins carried the casket to the cemetery. People asked, "Where was the fourth son to carry the father's body?" I would have given anything to have been there, along with my brothers taking him to his last resting place.

I told my mother how sorry I was that I had missed the opportunity. "You know, your father always missed you. He kept saying that if anything happened to him and you were not here, to make sure that I'll put your picture in his pocket by his heart when he was buried."

I never felt so moved; my father still humbled me after his death.

As we approached the cemetery that I had seen so many times before, I had a strange feeling. I never thought I would be visiting my father there.

"Stefanos, here is our son. He came to see you," my mother said with tears in her eyes.

The ground was fresh from digging the day before. I sat down and looked at his graveside; I wanted to see through the earth that separated me from him. I talked to my father for a long time. I told him where I had been and what I had done. I told him about his grandchildren that he had only seen in pictures. "I am sorry," I kept saying over and over.

Just before leaving the cemetery, I promised him that I would visit him more often. Passing the other graves on the way out, I read familiar names on the headstones. Every name brought memories of happier times of my childhood years growing up in my beloved city. The cemetery was peaceful; tall pine trees dispersed a soft shade on those who laid there. That was a right place for my father, quiet and serene. He could finally rest well there after his lifetime of hard work. I passed the gravesides of my uncles and those of my grandparents. My father was not too far from them.

That night as I lay in bed, I envisioned myself old with gray hair as if I was waiting to go away to a more peaceful world. My heart felt like a calm sea under the moonlight of a warm August night. My emotions were peaceful but contrasting.

I thought of the adventurous world, where I ran through most of my life; people with different colored skin, others with strange languages, and many with unfamiliar customs. I passed through busy highways, frozen streets, hot deserts and walked under the shadows of skyscrapers.

Nowhere was the familiar sea breeze of my hometown and there was no gardenias and jasmine on the streets. No people were arguing on the sidewalks or relaxing on the outdoor cafes. They were running, and I began to run with them, not knowing where I was going. I was curious to see their destination. We passed schools, churches, empty fields, stadiums, and beautiful homes.

Not many people stopped as if there was no destination at all. We passed seniors who were moving slowly and ran over young children who couldn't walk fast enough. It did not matter who we passed as long as we passed someone to get to the front of the line and leave behind the young and old.

In the years to come, especially after the death of my mother, and as I began to write down my thoughts, I searched for a word in English to define the love that remains after someone dear to you is gone. I know in my native language, as is in every language, there are many untranslatable words. Periodically, the urge to find such word, surfaced in my thoughts until I discovered it; Saudade. The Portuguese use it in many songs to trigger a lingering memory of someone who is an integral part of yourself, someone who brought joy in your life, and you are sad because that person is gone but happy because is still part of you. It is an absolutely potent word that makes me think of my parents and smile.

Saudade: When the past is profound and the present aspiring.

Besides my Grandmother who introduced me to Holiness, my Father who infused me with Wisdom and Justice and my Mother who taught me about Strength and Temperance, there were a few more people who defined my early life's characteristics. Among the many individuals who taught me invaluable lessons, there are two who are no longer with us.

My oldest brother Lefteris – Leadership, Ingenuity

My brother in law and best friend, Stavros – Humor, Civility.

My Heroes, My Town

20

THE PARK

I never had such a heavy heart's cry as I did during that period of trying to recover my strength. It was a time that I was trying to endure a world I couldn't comprehend. Never had I experienced this great anguish of being torn between two different cultures, two different philosophies, two different lifestyles. It was a schizophrenic tormenting of the mind, one side pulling back, and another side pushing to the forefront. Two different worlds: one that I loved, the other I must learn to like. So severely did my old wounds began to inflame as I followed my tracks, as I tried to leave behind the past and start the new. What an unimaginable torment of the soul.

To whom could I talk? Who would be willing to listen? Indeed, not people whose lives were consumed with their difficulties and overwhelmed with anxiety and responsibilities.

As I strolled around the water, to gather my thoughts, I felt a few shadows join my walk. We proceeded in silence, side by side.

The sun was going down. A brilliant sky appeared beyond the thin clouds in the west.

The chill of the evening covered the atmosphere, penetrating my bones, into my heart.

The shadows identified themselves as people whom I loved.

I had wrestled before with many of them. With some of them about severe ideological disagreements, and with others, while growing up, about lifestyle and antithetical choices. I must admit; I didn't understand their wisdom then.

With the familiar shadows by my side, I had begun my battle, trying to match the unmatchable. I wanted to reconcile utmost hope with absolute despair; to open a door beyond reason and certainty.

I took walks often, by the lake, in the park, between the trees, by the water, anywhere I could be isolated from the suffocating days of interacting with the masses of people.

The shadows came along to accompany me; there was a different one every time.

Father, mother, grandmother, and anyone who would listen, who would understand.

That day I needed them the most because it was impossible to make sense of the world surrounding me.

That day in the park was the beginning of winter. I was tired and sat on a bench. Children were playing and laughing, and parents were watching.

Suddenly the sky turned black. The wind picked up strength. The air filled with terror, roaring from the south, like a bloodthirsty tiger.

Mothers picked up their children and ran to safety.

The wind raged, bending trees, blowing leaves, whistling across the top of the water.

The entire city shook.

In the midst of the destruction, a shadow appeared. It walked towards the bench where I was sitting, stepping steadily against the wind, tall, powerful. It sat next to me. I gazed into the piercing eyes, the strong face, and the well-trimmed mustache.

"Father, the winter is here," I whispered. "Is that what you wanted for me?"

His face was serious as his voice spoke out loud, demanding and sorrowful, "Yes."

I could feel his heartbeat.

"I know what you're thinking. The winter will not stay for long and spring is next."

I saw a smile on his face.

The darkness of the sky had closed in on the earth.

Another shadow approached. It was thin, frail, walking stubbornly against the wind.

"Grandmother, you?"

Her wrinkled hands held mine, and peace overcame my heart.

"The spring is near," the voice descended from deep inside of me, demanding, relieved and clear.

I was alone again. I rose from the bench to leave. My life carried large and small joys and occasional sorrows. Sometimes I felt wounded, but most of the time I was caressed.

Habitual everyday affairs had left me. Now I knew I must learn to leave them too. It was not worth the trouble to turn back and hunt the elusive. I knew I could only chase the unknown, the future. The world would lose absolutely nothing if my contact with my contemporaries were to be about superficial indulgence.

Even if I fail to understand people and I look at them with contempt. Even if some don't deserve compassion. I must learn to like them all but love only a few.

The shadows walking with me asked me not to hate anyone,

to try to cope with everything along the way. Not to feel guilty if I harm people without desiring to do so.

My wish was to deliver myself, and as many others as possible, from mediocrity and boredom, to push toward greatness. Greatness in people entices me.

The voices of the shadows swirling in my head remind me of this. My mother's voice is the strongest.

And so, the shadows follow me everywhere, in the most critical moments of my life, like the ones in the park, when I was standing on the crossroads without any direction and determined to find a new path.

That day in the park I welcomed the strong wind striking my face.

It was the same wind that had scared the mothers, anxious to get their frightened children to safety. That day I decided that it was time for me to receive all struggles and welcome all hopes, to bring about order on my own, without accepting anyone's help. I would seek help only from those who had transformed their souls into shadows and followed my steps.

"The spring is near! I heard, I know it now."

My mind was awakened, my heart was not tormented, and nothing was trembling.

Out of the park, I went onto the crossroads. I did move on – in what direction? I genuinely do not remember. The course was important back then, but it does not matter now. It worked out anyway!

All I had to do was a simple thing; to discover what constitutes man's duty.

Some of the mysteries in life are incomprehensible to me. Like the human soul that ignites for an instant, and then bursts in the air, into myriads of bright flares, like a beautiful pyrotechnic, and then it vanishes. Who gave life such fascination and beauty and then suddenly, piteously, blows it up to the heavens, to black chaos full of silence?

When I left the crossroads, I knew that gradually and with unsure steps, I was about to walk into life's challenges. My soul was still unsettled, and my heart had just begun to challenge my destiny with courage and optimism.

At times, my repose and assurance were short-lived, as new doubts and anxieties sprang forth. But always, a new struggle delivered me from my former conviction to find a new one. The transformation was simple, out of a real maturity came another doubt.

One thing I know for sure, I had decided to go through my life without whining, pleading, or begging. This is what I wanted the most in my life. If this was against anyone's wishes, let it be.

For me, a park represents peaceful life; the trees, water sprinkling, children playing, adults relaxing, and dogs running free. It is where I daydream to escape from reality.

There was once this beautiful park, clad with green trees and fragrant plants. Hundreds of people were walking and playing. Flags of different colors wave in the air. On the one end of the park, accordions played sounds of sweet melodies. On the other end, colorful bands filled the air with magical music; there were hands clapping and sing-a-longs. Fireworks lighten the skies, careless children playing, teenage boys were talking to smiling girls.

It was a festive atmosphere in this park full of life. I wandered around that park; I was young and spirited. I saw people walking unafraid, with smiling faces and slow steps.

Many years later, aged and weary, I returned to that park. It was nightfall and the park was void of joy. A few dark clouds hung above my head. Gangs have replaced the happy children. Gunshots sounded from afar.

The colorful park was now inhospitable. The peaceful faces have become stark images.

In front of the park, teenagers listening to loud, angry songs and speak words of filth.

Torrential rains began to fall, erasing the images of yesteryear. Even the trees were leafless, and the plants have become brown sticks. There was sadness in my heart.

The big colorful park that once existed in my childhood is now barren and small.

How did we get so messed up?

Broken down doors, meaningless graffiti on walls, awful gunshot sounds in the night.

I questioned myself if this was reality or my perspective has changed with the passing of time. Time has traveled so fast, too fast, and life seems to last no longer than a desert flower. One that blossoms at the sunrise and withers at sunset.

My mind guided me around my childhood home. My heroes are no longer here. Their pictures on the walls generated love and wisdom, welcoming me back. It seems that memories and principles were frozen in time in the old house. I realized that I was wrong to see the park of life from a different perspective, for its darkness and not to rejoice for what is. I was fortunate to have answers to my curiosity as a child, but those kids in the park were growing up with thousands of unanswered questions, with no guidelines.

I glanced one last time around the house. My family was no

longer there. I have guilty feelings because I have let the years go by and missed so many memories with them.

I look in the mirror and I see the reflection of that little boy, smiling and ready to come out and play. I look at my siblings standing by me; a certainty that siblings should always be there for one another. Arguments and disagreements between us, no longer have any meaning.

In my last glance, nostalgic tears try to push out from my eyes. On the wall are icons of the saints my grandmother assured me they will be my protectors in life. There are pictures of countrysides that I admired, photographs of my parents and my children, people that I love so much, and there are mixed feelings of guilt and happiness.

I had lost the beautiful countryside through the travel on the muddy waters. For a while, winds rise, and angry waves pounded on me mercilessness. I challenged myself through lightning and thunderous skies.

I've seen that ship swallowed by the herculean waves. Nothing was scarier than that.

Now, I was certain that it was my fault to see the world through my weary eyes. Sleep escaped me that night. Excitement and revelations kept me awake.

As the sun erased the darkness of the night, I made a promise to rejoice every morning, as if it was a new life, a new beginning, and leave the bitterness behind. Thankfully, the shadows did not abandon me. They followed me throughout my life, and when needed they guided me back into the beautiful park.

My Heroes, My Town

21

MISPLACED

The room was full of smoke and I felt nauseated, but I had to endure that awful odor in the name of winning. I looked at the five people sitting around the table. Their faces had been in front of me for over twenty-four hours. The cards seemed like they were floating on the table as if it was part of a dream. My eyes were hurting from being open for so long. My mind could not comprehend anything but the numbers and the faces on the cards. My clothes reek of smoke and my face needed a good shave. The other people sitting at the table looked like they barely could keep their eyes open, but we kept on playing.

I remember the scene well because those years it happened often. In the casinos for poker tournaments or in someone's home for home games. From Las Vegas to Los Angeles and Phoenix, wherever there was an important game, I wanted in.

I disillusioned myself into thinking that this was just a job. The fact is that I loved the challenge of the game. The poker table was always kind to me. I was winning to the point that I would no longer get invitations to some home games. I spoke to some of my friends who had an ordinary but steady job, they thought that the profession of a gambler was a glamorous one. It wasn't. Contrary to the general belief that it takes luck to win, poker is a game of skills; a game that involved mathematics, psychology and self-restraint. There is no doubt that gambling is an addiction but at least with poker, you have control over your actions. 'What kind of life is this?' I often thought. Especially when I introduced myself as a professional gambler and people looked at me with contempt. Those were the days before successful poker players became superstars.

In life, we make the mistake of disapproving the lifestyles of others and we are critical about their beliefs. We admire various talented people and we want to be like them, while we condemn others without fully knowing them. I believe that everyone has a secret life, and a private one, and of course a public personality. It is impossible to comprehend a person, therefore illogical to judge. It is naive to believe in everything and everyone. My logic tells me if I believe in everything and everyone then it is a metaphor for believing in nothing. And those who believe in nothing are cynics. It is that simple.

As long as there are greed and addictions, there will be truckloads of drugs carrying death. As long there is ignorance, there will be child abuse and disrespect for the elders. As long there is poverty and injustices, there will be a crime. The belief that violence could accomplish peace is an oxymoron; how is that a person does not understand that?

I remember the times when I was lost in life's temptations. I lived in uncertainty; it was like an unstoppable roller-coaster ride, uncertain of where or when it would stop. I realized that if I did not have the power to prevent a terrible ride, I should not get on it at all.

Once I had a strange dream; where the earth lost its course. It was like a colossal dryer floating people and things in slow motion. When the turning stopped, all objects had landed in odd places unfamiliar to one another.

There was graffiti of swastika flags on building walls. People were waving banners with images of Bin Laden, Mussolini and Nero. Hurry up. Let's stir this earth one more time. Things and people spun once more. And when it stopped, more strange things appeared. Nobody helped the blind man who had lost his white cane. Wealthy preachers were speaking about greed being a sin. People slept on the sidewalks. Bullets are killing our heroes and inspirations. Where is John? Where is Bobby? Where is Martin? Money was buying friendships and administrations, and guns, and tanks, and nuclear weapons. The earth was being destroyed; burning forests, garbage on the streets. The immigrants are now children of a lesser god. Children are taken away from their mothers and refugees are drowning in the sea. But, by any means let's keep telling people that all is fine. I was anticipating in one of those spins that someone would take away the microphones from the politicians and give them to the comedians. But, no matter how many times the earth spun around some things remain the same.

I admit that I have an addiction; I can't rest if things are not right, and I cannot follow instructions I do not agree with. I have had this problem since I was a child. I've always wanted to live my life the way that makes sense to me and not the way that people want me to; to follow my truth without offending others. To some people, the truth is insulting and bothersome. But, to me, insulting is poverty, hunger, and abuse.

I mean, listen to some of the world's political leaders; they lie without consequences.

Guns in the schoolyards. Children run for safety through

forests, and on makeshift boats to cross the seas. Global warming and pollution are destroying our earth.

Hunger strikes. Peace walks. Street fights. What happened to the old movies?

Bank robberies. Military invasions. Terrorists bomb the buildings. All that brings sadness to my heart.

The uprising of the rebels, doubtful leaderships, political corruption, abused democracy.

Children are starving around the world. Students are executed in schools for no reason, religious wars, political assassinations. Children are giving birth to babies. Mothers are killing their children. How did the refugees have become society's open wound?

I wonder when all this is going to stop?

Something is eating up my heart. Something is bringing tears to my eyes.

But, something is keeping me hopeful that the good someday will prevail.

I know, I know, I should follow my theory about life; Make the bad memories into lessons and rejoice on the good memories. There are plenty of those.

After this strange dream, I kept awake for the rest of the night. My mind took me on a journey to the past, in which I was reminded of things and places that have been forgotten by the passing of time; muted by the busy work schedule and life's ongoing responsibilities.

The early years when I fell in love with music and the movies, Piaf and Aznavour were already legends. Bogart was cool in Casablanca, and Loren with Mastroianni were breaking hearts

Elvis went to his Heartbreak Hotel to revolutionize music,

and Cassius Clay proclaimed that he was the greatest.

The Beatles were saying, "All you need is love."

Protesters on the streets, demanded equal rights.

Gandhi said, "An eye for an eye will leave the world blind."

It was about that time that my father decided that Athens was where I would continue my education.

Pele was pure magic. Hippies are everywhere. Let's save the forests.

"Get off my counter," whites say to blacks. Love, not war baby! Peace signs are everywhere.

The Stones want satisfaction. Aretha demands respect, Pickett is riding his '67 Mustang. Mandela begins his incredible journey. Who is paying attention?

Then I injured my right ankle - that wasn't good. But, it forced me to explore other possibilities. To get away, to set sail to see the world, to find a new excitement. The different cultures fascinated me and intrigued my imagination.

On I went, traveling from one end of the world to another, to escape from reality, using the marine merchant ships as my means of transportation and a source of income.

I found myself walking on the streets of Astoria in New York where a sizable Greek population thrived in a beehive of ethnic groceries, restaurants, and small shops. Some of the Greeks I met were trying to keep me there, "You can work in the kitchen, and make a lot of money, maybe someday you'll have your own business," they said, and I laughed. "What? Are you crazy? I was not about to waste my life in the kitchens, in the markets, or wherever there is work. I have places to go, people to see, and a life to live. No thanks. Little that I knew decades later I would be doing the same thing I despised back then.

It was time for me to join the army. Images of war everywhere, flower children dancing on the streets.

Men are blown to pieces in the rice paddies. Draft dodgers, peace marches, violent demonstrations. Nixon claims that he is not a crook. Castro is mocking the world. Bond, James Bond, saves the day.

Americans think of Mexicans as enemy number one! The Eagles check into the Hotel California. Bandannas, Rock and roll, and Woodstock. The second Apollo lands on the moon.

Shaved heads clad in yellow robes nagging everyone in the airport terminals. James Dean lives, and McQueen is cool. The Russians are breeding baby Gorbachev.

Students revolt but they are gunned down on the campus of Athens Polytechnic. Kissinger, not the poor Mexicans, is enemy number one.

And then...silence. Zeal and idealism were lost in the responsibility of work and family.

22

THE GAMBLER

As the sun descended behind the hills into a horizon of multitude brilliant colors, another day of work ended for the team trying to rebuild the ruined homes. Near the end of my military duty, I was part of a team helping to repair or rebuild the damaged infrastructure. My group of about eighty personnel was rebuilding the earthquake-destroyed village of Ladiko, a community in the northern part of Peloponnese.

Within months, the servicemen lifted new structures from the rubbles. Soon there will be homes for people to return to from their temporary camps, a school for the children, a square for people to socialize, and a church to worship. I was one of the first to arrive at this camp. We setup oversize tents, a small kitchen and an office. My job was to keep the bookkeeping for our captain and do the shopping for groceries from the nearby village. This military division was thought to be a hard-labor camp; individuals who were marked as rebellious were sent here from the Army, Navy or Air Force to do heavy construction work. However, most of us thought that this camp was like a holiday resort. We were away from the strict daily military schedule, and uniform codes. After the initial setup, more members of the armed forces joined us in groups, a few at a time. In one of those arrivals, there was Andreas Frangoulis, whom I served with in Serres and we had become good friends.

After work, we use to walk to the nearby village where Andreas, the tall, good-looking athlete, was very popular among the female population and had received several offers for marriage. But Andreas' dream was to go to America. Soon after he was released from the military, he was on an airplane flying to America.

In Chicago, he was reunited with his father and sister who lived in a populated Greek neighborhood. At the age of twenty-four, Andreas had fulfilled his dream; he was in America, a foreign world, one that he soon realized was not what he had anticipated.

His sister was married with two children and moved in with his father who lived alone.

Andreas had not seen his father for twelve years and he rarely saw him when he got to Chicago. His father left for work before sunrise and came home late at night.

Andreas worked nights at a restaurant as a dishwasher and went home in the early morning hours. In the few hours Andreas spent with his father, he realized that this was not the same man he knew as a twelve-year-old boy back in the village.

The new lifestyle was frantic and monotonous, confined to work, sleep, and more work. The sun was nowhere to be found and the air was musty. There was snow everywhere and the people who lived under the ominous atmosphere were irritable and isolated into their homes. Andreas was confined between piles of dirty dishes, pots and pans. At the end of the week, he received a handful of dollars, a modest payment for his constant sweat and aching feet.

There was no time for church on Sunday, for coffee with friends, or a movie.

This new world, this new life was extreme and cruel, but Andreas never complained. He worked harder so his aging father could work less. He was determined to adopt this new world, to learn all that was possible about this new culture.

Silent waves of pain roared inside of him. However, soon Andreas began to find his way, to escape from the cultural exile, and he began to appreciate the offerings of his new home. Chicago was a city that I ended up in as well. At first, I was trying to make a living playing soccer, not a popular sport in the early seventies in America. Eventually, to survive, I was sold Good Humor ice cream out of a small truck. After a game of soccer came, the team went to a pizza place for dinner. This is where I saw Andreas again. After a brief conversation and plans to be connected, we separated once again. The last thing he said to me was, "I am planning to go to Alaska to work on the pipelines. Do you want to go?"

The thought of the freezing weather in Alaska made me shiver. I was pushing my limits of weather-acceptance in Chicago. "No to Alaska. Thanks, my friend."

Many years later, I was walking out from the Las Vegas International Airport and I rushed among the masses of visitors toward the taxicab line. A young couple rushed by me, laughing, seduced by the magic of the sorceress city with the phantasmagoric lights. They approached the taxicab I was supposed to take as they were hugging, kissing and laughing. For a moment I thought, how nice it is to laugh and drink and dance.

I stood by the sidewalk, once again captivated by the people's apprehensive faces, people anxious to get to the heart of the city, to toss their belongings in their rooms and rush down to be a part of the impulsive energy of gambling and entertainment. My trips to Las Vegas were frequent during those years. It was there that I felt a certain aspect of coolness. It was intriguing to be friendly with numerous nameless people who, in an instant, became strangers again.

Once the swarm of people thinned out a bit, I entered one of the taxicabs.

"Downtown," I said.

The driver weaved his car around the heavy airport traffic and headed toward the strip.

I looked outside, captivated by the rapid changes. Every time I visited this city, there was something new. Innovative, colossal buildings sprang from the earth to tower up to the gambling heavens.

"Are you staying for a while?" the driver asked.

"A few days," I answered to be polite.

"Obviously this is not your first time in Vegas – Right?" he continued his questioning.

"Right," I said.

As he continued to talk, I sensed a familiarity with his accent.

I glanced at his rear-view mirror. He looked at me through the mirror and smiled.

"Are you here for business or fun?" His voice came across with an ironic manner.

"I am thinking to enter a poker tournament at the Horseshoe," I answered.

"Really!" he exclaimed, still glancing at me through his mirror, smiling.

"Do I know you?" My curiosity about this man was

now evident.

"Of course, we know each other, very well," he proclaimed. I looked at his taxi license hanging by the money meter and my eyes opened widely.

"Andreas is that you?"

He turned around and smiled, "How easily we forget our friends!" he said with sarcasm.

He pulled his cab into a parking lot. "Let's get a bite to eat," He said.

Standing in front of me, he looked so different. He was much thinner, he had lost most of his hair, and he did not stand erect. There was not much resemblance in this aging man to the tall, athletic young man that I once knew.

We sat at a table in a small diner.

It was peculiar to sit across from someone you know but do not recognize. Perhaps the environment, the civilian clothes, and the circumstances, in general, forced me to look at him through a different lens.

"You haven't changed much," he said. Even his voice was different; it sounded hesitant and discolored.

"You have," I responded.

Andreas bowed his head as if he was ashamed.

"What happened to you, what are you doing in Las Vegas, driving a cab?"

He looked at me. "I told you I was going to Alaska?"

I scrambled my brains, trying to understand how this dramatic change of a person was possible. "What happened to you, Andreas?"

"It's a long story," he mumbled.

"I have time," I said.

"You know, my dream was to come to America."

"I know, I know."

"When I arrived in Chicago everything was so different than I had imagined."

He went on to tell me that the excitement to be in America eventually faded away in the dish-washing room of a restaurant where endless loads of dirty dinnerware keep piling higher while he worked countless hours for very little money. "My cousin, Markos – Did I ever tell you about him?"

"I don't think so."

"Well, Markos was going to Alaska. He heard that there were plans to build roads and a pipeline from one end of the state to another. Markos told me that there would be a lot of work in Alaska and that the pay was good. I thought for a while and decided that anything was better than what I was doing. A few days after I saw you in the pizza place in Chicago, we got into his car and headed to the northwest." Andreas went on to tell me the story.

The two cousins drove Markos' 1958 Chrysler Imperial, through Iowa, South Dakota, Montana and Idaho, and because of car problems, they reached Seattle after an episodic four-day drive. In Seattle, Markos sold his old car and they boarded the bus to Bellingham, the seaport town north of Seattle.

From Bellingham, they embarked on the ferry to Juneau, a voyage with spectacular scenery of islands, fjords, fishing villages and with the occasional presence of eagles and whales. The ferry arrived at their destination three days later. From Juneau, Andreas and Markos, traveled by train to Fairbanks. During the trip to Fairbanks, they had the opportunity to see the spectacular views of majestic mountains, hurtling waterfalls, lush forests and unique towns. In Fairbanks, the two cousins found an agent who recruited them for work. With several others, they were taken by bus to the north with their destination of Prudhoe Bay. The construction of the road from Prudhoe Bay to Yukon River had just begun.

In less than a year the three-hundred-sixty-mile road was completed and the workers who helped build the road returned south to unite with thousands of others to start the construction of the pipeline that had begun in Tonsina River, just north of Valdez.

When the two cousins arrived in Alaska it was the beginning of summer, the weather was warm and the greenery entirely brilliant. The environment was a pleasant surprise to them, since Alaska exemplified, in their minds, unbearably cold and gloomy skies. But the pleasantries of the atmosphere were soon spoiled by the winter; a winter that created an intolerable working situation, forcing the workers into an inhumane living. The bitter frostiness and depressing skies became a constant companion for the two cousins as they moved from camp to camp.

The further north the construction of the pipeline shifted, the worst the weather conditions grew to be. Life in the pipeline camps was harsh and exhausting for the thousands of workers who came to Alaska during the construction to seek adventure and fortune. The camps were crammed with people and privacy was a luxurious component. The two cousins were inseparable and protected one another - until a haunting night of tragedy.

Their camp had moved north. The cold weather delayed the delivery of parts needed for the workers to continue their work. Some of the workers were given a rare two-days off as they were waiting for the parts to arrive. The two cousins decided to go to Fairbanks and visit the section of town along Second Avenue, the home of rowdy bars, prostitutes and drugs.

Andreas and Markos squeezed into space at the bar of the smoke-filled, alcohol-reeking saloon where the noise was raucous and the mood unruly. It was past midnight as two of the client-seeking women approached the two cousins. The four of them talked and they laughed until four big, beard-clad men walked towards the two couples and demanded that the women go with them. The town was overflowing with visitors and there were not enough women to satisfy the desire of flesh-craving men.

The four rowdies, starving for the scent of a woman, we're not going anywhere without their bounty. The two cousins tried to reason with them but when alcohol takes over, the mind is unruly.

"Come on buddy we don't want any trouble," smooth-talking Markos tried to talk his way out. The tongue-incoherent-giants ignored him.

Andreas was a giant of a man as well but next to the four hulking men he did not look so massive.

One of the bearded men grasped the hand of the woman standing next to Markos. She pulled back. Even a prostitute has a choice of her companionship.

Comparing the alcohol-scented beast with the clean-cut, good-looking Markos, left her with not much of choice. But choices sometimes are cruel.

The hairy giant was offended and grasped the woman's hand again. She pushed his hand away and told him to get lost.

The three other friends, sensing the excitement, stepped closer to the two couples. It was apparent that they did not want to leave without taking the women with them.

The two cousins glanced at each other; they were ready to

back away; it wasn't worth the trouble.

And then, it all happened so fast; there was not much of an exchange of words. The hairy giant pulled a knife and stabbed Markos repeatedly. Andreas tried to save his cousin, but he was overpowered and beaten.

Markos dropped, his blood spilling on the dirty saloon floor. The music kept playing at full volume, people kept drinking and the four giants walked out without the women.

The two women, shocked for a moment, found the strength to let out screams for help. It was then that the patrons paid attention to the two humans on the floor, one dead the other bloody and injured. Andreas went into a deep depression after his cousin's death.

Markos did not have any siblings, just a mother living in Greece who he took care of by sending her money. Andreas kept working until there was no more work for him.

A year after Markos' murder, the eight hundred miles of Alaskan pipeline project was finished. The pipeline stretched, in and above the Alaskan ground, like an enormous snake twisting and turning over three mountain ranges, from the southern port of Valdez to the northern slope of Alaska.

Andreas' dream to come to America for a better life was not a reality. Now he wanted to go back to Greece. He packed his bags ready for his return.

Andreas remembered the many times that Markos told him, "when we are done with this hard work in Alaska we are going to Las Vegas to celebrate in style." Las Vegas had an exciting ring to Andreas' ears and before boarding the plane to Greece, he made a spontaneous visit to Las Vegas; the mythical city that he had heard so much about. Andreas arrived in Las Vegas with over a quarter of a million dollars. He booked a hotel for one week on the Las Vegas Strip. During that week the solitude and murkiness of Alaska channeled into the clamor and the bright lights of the magical city.

Andreas tried the roulette wheel first and when he lost some money there, he decided to get even by shooting craps. The dice were not friendly to him either and he lost a lot more. He thought that he was going to get his money back at the poker table, but poker is not for the fainthearted who want to make fast money. His last attempt to make up his losses was at the blackjack table where money disappear fast.

Once a gambler reaches that kind of desperation, his soul belongs to the gods of gambling.

23

POINT OF RETURN

The week in Las Vegas became months and the months, turned into years, and the years reduced the strong young man with the triumphant smile into an old man driving a cab to earn some money, to return to a casino. The notion that someday he would win back all his money and hold his fortune in his hands again is once unrealistic and addictive.

When I met my friend in Las Vegas, he had arrived there from Alaska five years ago.

The earnings from driving a taxi were not enough to support his gambling addiction. He started borrowing money from friends and loan sharks.

Unable to pay back the money, the friends became enemies and the loan sharks seriously dangerous. His gambling addiction had taken over reason and responsibility.

Andreas lived in a little run-down apartment furnished with just a bed to sleep and a table to eat. He lived with a girl named Carol.

We went to his apartment the day I met him in Las Vegas and when he sensed my disappointment in him, he proclaimed, "Things are tough. I am trying to make a living!"

I said nothing for I knew his misery was enough retribution for his addiction.

His friend Carol was unkempt, but polite nevertheless. She sat quietly in the corner of the room while Andreas and I spoke about the past.

"I want to go back to Greece after I win my money back," he proclaimed.

"I think you have to face reality. The chances of winning back your money is a very remote possibility. Your best bet is to go back to your home in Greece and get a fresh start there."

"No, no, I am going to do it. I will win everything back, you'll see."

While in Las Vegas, I devoted most of my time to following Andreas from one casino to another, chasing his elusive dream. For his part, he wanted to show me that he was capable of winning back his money.

Three days after my arrival in Las Vegas I was ready to go back. He drove me to the airport. When we arrived at the airport, he stepped out of his cab and we stood by the sidewalk.

"I hope to see you soon," he said.

I looked at him and shook my head.

"What?" he asked.

"You know what," I answered.

"It's not what you think," he tried to find the reasoning for his lifestyle.

"What is it then?"

He bent his head and scratched his forehead.

"You see all these," he said pointing to the intimidating building, to the lights, to the people flocking the streets, "all this glamor, all this energy?" he continued.

Then he looked me in the eyes and said, "I'll rather spend three years working under inhumane conditions in Alaska than one year living like this in Las Vegas." His eyes were misty.

"You know what to do then," I said.

"Yeah, I know what to do," he repeated.

I pulled out whatever money I had in my pocket and I placed it in his hand.

"What is this?" he asked.

"I overheard Carol saying that it was time to pay the rent," I said.

"Absolutely not," he tried to insist that he wouldn't take the money.

"Keep the money. You know you need it to pay your rent. So long, my friend."

"I'll come to see you in Phoenix."

"Anytime."

As the airplane ascended to the clear skies, I looked down. The casinos resembled little doll-houses, and the people like ants had taken over the streets, crawling into every open door. A year after meeting Andreas in Las Vegas, I had opened my first restaurant, from where I began my odyssey in the restaurant universe. My trips to Las Vegas and home poker games had ended. A new chapter had entered my life and my passion for creating new recipes was now materialized. People packed the hallway of my tiny restaurant and lined up all the way outside the door. Servers rushed to pick up the dishes coming out of the kitchen, to serve the guests, and to keep up the frantic pace. The temperature outside was approaching triple digits, an indication that summer was around the corner in Phoenix.

One day Andreas rushed his way through the waiting line of people, walked by the hostess' desk and stood in front of the open kitchen. I looked at him through the endless food orders hanging from the kitchen's ticket wheel. His face was full of anxiety, like a man on the run, a man who knows his hunters are a few steps behind him. "I need help," he said.

"You've got to wait. Go to the back room, have some lunch, we'll talk later," I said, anxious to return to my work.

"I know you are busy, but it is urgent. I need to see you as soon as possible."

"Just go in the back and wait." I glanced at the door; the line of people had shortened. Among the people was Ted, a character who always reminded me of the actor Joe Pesci

"What is he doing here?" I asked.

"He is just giving me a ride."

Ted was a con artist; he would tell any sad story to anyone to hustle gambling money.

"I am desperate. I have to run away from Las Vegas." Andreas said with urgency in his voice.

"Have something to eat. We'll talk after the lunch rush. Give him something to eat too," I said pointing at Ted.

The two of them devoured their lunch in the back kitchen. Lunchtime passed, and the restaurant was soon empty.

"Let's take a ride," I told Andreas.

We drove around the streets of Phoenix without a direction, to get away and talk.

It was hot, the kind of blistering heat that makes you want to lay in a tub full of ice cubes and your mind yearns for deep sea waters and cool mountain tops.

We talked about old times; we laughed and lamented about

the notable adventures of the past. We reminisced about the dreams we had when we were younger and how everything had turned out so differently. And we expressed satisfaction knowing that the military generals, those who defined our life's path are now rotting in jail.

"What do you want to do now, Andreas?" I asked.

A shade of nostalgia draped his eyes.

"I don't want to live like this anymore. I want to escape this tormenting life. I feel trapped." His voice was distressing.

The road led us to Sky Harbor Airport.

"Do you really want to get away from all this?" I asked.

"Yes, I do," he said firmly.

We sat silently in the cool lobby of the airport, watching people rushing in and out of the terminals.

"Do you have your passport with you?"

"Everything I possess is here," he said pointing to a duffel bag he carried with him.

Then he turned and stared at me; he did not have to say anything as his facial expression said it all.

"Well, I thought you wanted to get away," I said.

"You mean right now?"

"Why not?"

"But, I just can't leave like that!"

"Listen to me; I believe that the best thing for you to do now is to go, to leave everything behind you. The money from Alaska is never coming back. Go to Greece for a fresh start in life."

"I don't know; I don't know... I thought of going back – but suddenly just like that, without planning?"

My old friend was a man at the crossroads; he knew that moving on was the right thing to do, but the dazzling lights of

Las Vegas had been implanted in his psyche.

"Look, I've known you at your best and I've seen you at your worst. It was back in our country that you were at your best. Going back is not just the right thing - it is the only thing."

He looked at me for a moment, seemingly trying to digest what I had said.

"Maybe you are right. But I have nothing…"

"You have learned to survive after the ordeal in the military, in Chicago, and Alaska. We all have learned to survive."

He glanced at me; his expression was doubtful; lips pressed together and said, "I am not sure if I can go back to the simple life of the village."   "A simple life is better than no life," I told him.

We stood in front of the ticket counter. I bought him a ticket to Athens via New York.

"Now, don't get off in New York the same way you did in Las Vegas. Keep on going," I reminded him.

"No, I made that mistake once. I want to go back," he said with a tone of relief in his voice.

We walked to the gate. It was time to go; it was time for him to escape the misery.

And, it was time for me to dream about the refreshing blue waters of the Aegean Sea. I wished I was going with him. We embraced. He was emotional.

"You planned this – didn't you?" he asked.

"No, not really. You know me I don't usually make long-term plans."

I placed a handful of money in his hand. He hung his head with embarrassment.

As I watched him walk with tired steps toward the gate, I

could not help wondering what became of the young Hercules I once knew, what happened to his spirit?

Once he was the gentle lion that roared at the enemies of freedom. Life had tripped him over and tossed him into a labyrinth full of sirens and unbeatable beasts. To many people, he was a hopeless gambler, a loser, but to those who knew him well, he would always be a hero.

I checked my watch. It was approaching five o'clock. I had to go back to the restaurant, to prepare for the dinner rush.

Ted was still in the restaurant entertaining the waitresses and the cooks.

"Welcome back," he said with a smile. Then he looked towards the front door.

"Where is Andreas?" he asked.

"He is going."

"Going where?"

"I have no idea, Ted. He asked me to stop the car at an intersection, and when I did, he opened the door and walked away."

"Walked away where…why did you let him go?"

"I begged him to get back to the car, but he wouldn't. He seemed pretty depressed."

Ted was in a panic mode.

"I have to find him," he said anxiously.

" Me too, I am afraid that he might do something crazy," I said.

Ted stood speechless for a moment. I could see it in his eyes that he was planning his next hustling move.

"What will I do now?" his voice was sad.

"What do you mean?"

"I mean, he was supposed to get money for gas, to drive back to Las Vegas."

"I don't know what to tell you. He is gone," just hoping he would go away.

But Ted, like a seasoned con artist, never gives in. If there were a kingdom of hustlers, he would have been the king.

He looked at me with a pathetic, desperate facial expression.

"Can you help out?" he asked.

"Ted, man, you are wearing an Armani summer suit, Ferragamo shoes and a Pierre Cardin shirt, and you are asking me, a working man, to give you money for gas?"

He went on to point out all his problems, the usual bad-luck-blame-others stories which I am sure he had repeated hundreds of times.

"I guess I could buy you lunch," I said smiling.

"Lunch? Come on; I need some gas money. I have money in Vegas; I'll send you the money when I get there."

"Yeah right!" I handed him a twenty-dollar bill. He looked at it and said, "That's not enough gas to get me there."

"That's enough for gas to get you to Kingman. I am sure you have some friends there."

"Man, you are cold."

"I know."

He pocketed the money, took some food to go and smiled as he was leaving.

On his way out, he hugged the waitress and waved goodbye to the cooks.

Then he walked out as the waitresses were telling him to come back soon.

But Ted was on his way to new acquaintances, those who

have not heard his stories before.

My Heroes, My Town

24

GRANDMOTHER

I closed my eyes. There was my mother's face weeping silently, without tears on her face, as I was leaving her behind once again to run from city to city, to explore the mysteries of the earth. On my father's face, I saw very little emotion. He was too wise to cry tears of separation. He knew that the world had no borders, that they were just lines on the ground that people had drawn to separate themselves from others. He knew the time had come to create my path, to seek my destiny and to find my universe. It was my grandmother who occasionally emerged silently amidst the chaos, to divulge her spirit, and remind me of the definition of humanity. Grandmother, it is you who taught me how to laugh and how to cry. I remembered the last time I spent time with you, there in your little chapel, in the mystic darkness, surrounded by the icons of your venerable saints. It was there, under the candlelight you burned for me, that I felt the touch of your kind heart. I still feel your touch in my hands, on my face, as I hear your voice telling me not to be afraid of the world. "How can you be afraid of something that you love?" you asked me once.

You told me to fight with love, courage and wisdom, never

with a rifle in hand, never with hatred and bloodshed. I have always smiled at your image, thinking how right you are, grandmother.

Back then I was a young bull, concerned with social morality and questioning hell, but you told me otherwise. You said to me that morality is for the guilty and hell is for those who fear consequences of their actions.

You once told me that the world is an enigma, elusive for mortals to resolve.

Later in life, I paraphrased your observation with the Chimera, a fire-breathing monster with a lion's head, a goat's body, and a serpent's tail. In other words, it is an illusory organism, imagined but impossible to be attained.

My journey, carrying unyielding beliefs, began there, in the company of your saints.

I remembered it was a hot August afternoon when I left once again to conquer the world and save humankind from evil.

Along the way, I found adventures, resistance, apathy, and adversity. I visited strange lands, and I saw others who had antithetical, unyielding beliefs as well.

It was during my travels that I began to comprehend the fire-breathing Chimera.

It was then that the sentiments of the world simultaneously swarmed around me. There were reality and fantasy, dialectics and logic, ideas and feelings, deceitfulness and convictions.

It was a time that I was everywhere and nowhere. It seemed to be an unending disconnect within myself and that created an enduring tribulation for myself. And before long I was in the realm of perpetual condemnation of myself.

You were one of the shadows that came to the park

that day and told me that the spring was near. Since then there have been many shadows that accompanied my walk in this enigmatic world.

As I lay on my bed, eyes closed and mind traveling, I remembered when you spoke of evil. You said that evil is a spirit, not a body and that evil could overtake our spirit but not the person.

In the middle of the night, when the Chimera is sleeping, and the senses are relaxed, it is then that I have visions.

It was a brilliant sundown, a warm day.

The calendar read the twenty-fifth day of an ambitious month. It was the sixth day of a busy week and the last month of the year. The end was near.

I remembered seeing my life passing by quickly, just like a movie in fast-forward mode, as if anxious to seek the next morning, move to the next adventure.

Between the morning and the sunset, several images faded, lost in the cruelty of time.

There were immeasurable pleasures, endless travels, praises, lies, victories and defeats.

In the afternoon, just before the brilliant sundown, I was walking down the street of an unknown town.

Thousands of people came and stood on the sidewalks and the balconies.

These people were cheering, and some were jeering. There was a panegyric atmosphere.

I recognized some of the faces in the crowd. There were schoolboys from my childhood, and the people I played soccer with. There were people whom I never met, people that I worked with and others who admired my work.

There I saw women I knew and the children I loved.

I was not sure what the commotion was all about? But I was uncomfortable with all the havoc.

I quickened my steps to get away from that street.

I moved away from the crowds with a victorious feeling, not because of the cheering crowd, but because I was leaving the noise and the pretense behind.

At this point, nothing from my past meant much, except the lessons I have learned.

The past was a land that I had conquered, a place in which I had lived for a while.

The crowd of people was thinning out and the noise of the city became a distant echo.

Alone at last! What a great relief it was.

Ahead of me, the bright orange sun appeared like an enormous fiery circle. The sky was like the canvas of a creative painter who had combined colors of rare origin: thick yellow, cherry pink, muted red, luminous orange, ruddy peach.

The sunlight was illuminating the mountaintops, up where free creatures, like the hawks and the eagles, built their burrows. I wish I could talk to them.

There was no one else to talk to, to confide my joys and my sorrows, to tell about youth's dreams and mystic yearning.

To whom should I relate to how many times I slipped and fell; how many times I rose and began again, once more to ascend?

I don't know if anyone cares to hear my confessions. I don't think anyone is interested in analyzing my fire-breathing Chimera.

The miles were left behind; the town was like a quick flash

of a camera, like life itself. In the city I left behind, nothing much had changed, except for new buildings sprouting from the earth, majestically, heavenward. These grand structures intimidate people and make them feel like ants. From inside the colossal structures, the masters call for people to enter, to trap them and enslave them.

"Come…Enter…Come…"

And the people cannot resist the sweet, seductive voices coming from the luxurious structures with the blinding lights.

Thousands, millions of people, hypnotized, obey the seductive voices. They enter the mouth of the siren seeking protection, riches, looking for pity.

I have heard those voices; they are irresistible.

I struggle to console my heart, to reconcile, to freely deny, to move away from the lights blinding my eyes, but the voice remains loud, reverberating in my ears.

"Come…come back…"

The heart beats inside my chest, resisting, crying.

"Come back…stay a little…enjoy…"

I threw a final glance back toward the lights. Their brightness was stubbornly wrestling with me. I smiled as I noticed that nothing has changed, yet nothing is like it used to be.

In the city of the lights, there are only a few masters that rule life; the rest must obey.

The masters have thrown the bait: unfulfilled promises, unrealistic dreams, and quixotic ideas, to draw in the timid, to make them crawl in. And the people fall into the trap of impossible expectations, of unfulfilled promises. Powerless and defeated, they stay to please the beast of dependency, to serve the masters.

I remembered, long ago, it was time for me to go, to get

out of the sorceress town, where hearts crack under the spell. I heard the voices, "Come back…please…don't go…"

Only I was fortunate to see beyond the seductive sounds.

"Take…take some more…credit cards, diamonds, elaborate homes, loans, expensive cars. Only you must stay to serve our greed; only you must obey our rules."

I smiled as I looked back. "Here, take it all" I offered, knowing that the Chimera would not be satisfied unless I was defeated, humiliated and begging.

The road ahead was lonely. The lights of the city dazzled in my memory, but further, I must walk.

Grandmother, the schooling in the phantasmagoric city is done. There is nothing to learn there anymore. I cast a final glance back. To whom should I say farewell; To what?

The countryside I walk upon is beautiful. There is nothing to blind me, only attractive natural structures, like the rugged mountains, the green valleys, and the blue seas.

Here, in a place away from the Chimera, is where you are liberated.

Grandmother, you told me that the world is enigmatic, not to try to untangle it, to wait for the spring.

Now I understand.

Nikos Ligidakis

Before the birth of my sister

25

THE JOURNEY

The people around her were speaking a strange language. There were signs with peculiar lettering, boisterous noises and humans hurrying by, created an unfamiliar scenery around her. It was just another day at the J.F.K. Airport in New York. But for her was a new experience. She had never been on an airplane before, and after the long flight from Athens, my mother was now walking in this hectic, chaotic airport. She was dressed in black, holding her black purse and slow stepping towards her terminal. Her legs prevented her from moving fast, they have been swollen for so many years now, but she always managed to get where she wanted to go. She started her long trip from Athens to Phoenix to see her son and her grandchildren. Considering the circumstances, it took remarkable courage to take that long journey. Her resolve was nothing new to me; It was one of the elements of her character that made her so impressive.

As I am thinking about my mother's unusual trip, I find a parallel with life's journey; about how the culture, the social structure and family interaction mold our individuality and fundamental principles of life. Here is my mother, an older woman, who lived a demanding life, through wars, poverty, birthing and raising five children while working hard, and not once did I hear despair in her voice. Amazing right?

And do you think she cared about walking around the lights and glamor of New York City wearing her black dress, without makeup or a fancy hairdo but looking so radiant and so beautiful? The proverb that says beauty comes from within, defines my mother. And my mother defines life. There is no way to describe a harmonious life in a few lines but here is what I learned from my mother's exemplary life; It wasn't the materialistic happiness or selfishness that brought joy in her life. It was the ordinary lifestyle that made her extraordinarily happy. And accepting the fact that grief and suffering are part of life while making the wellbeing of your family the centerpiece of your existence, made her a veritable saint in my eyes. I only regret that it took me so long to realize her virtues.

I remember one time she stopped the train for me.

I was in the service and I was being transferred from Athens to the city of Pyrgos. The train was to pass through my hometown of Kiato. Once my father learned this, he made a package for me with food and money. He asked my mother to go to the train station, wait for the train and give me the package. My mother was late and before she could get to the station, the train started to move. She stood on the railroad tracks and raised her hand, and with this gesture, the train stopped. The engineer, who knew my family, stepped out.

"Anastasia, what are you doing?" he asked.

"I must give this package to my son. He is on the train," she said.

"And you had to stop the train?" he replied surprised.

"Well, it is his father's wish," she said.

The engineer shook his head. He knew my father well.

Many passengers looked out of the train windows in curiosity as to why the train had stopped. I saw my mother standing there talking with the engineer.

"Mother, what are you doing here?" I asked.

"I brought a few things to take with you," she said handing me the package.

I was more embarrassed than impressed at the time.

"Take care of yourself. And don't forget to write often," she yelled as the train went on.

Now I feel guilty that I was embarrassed and not proud of her.

When we are young, we are so concerned about our self-image, we overlook the importance of how integrity and civility play a significant role in society.

Material possessions that give us temporary joys in life have been replaced with other, upgraded toys. But, it is the joy of the holidays and the sadness of death, the laughter of the children and smiles of the elders, the helping hand or the concern for others; it is those memories that shaped our substance.

My mother strolled through the J.F.K. airport in New York. She had missed her connecting flight to Phoenix. She spoke not one word of English, but that did not matter; it was not enough for her to panic. Arrangements were made from Athens by my sister, for mother to spend the night with one of her friends in New York. The next day my mother would catch a flight to Phoenix.

I couldn't wait to see her. I had not seen her for a long time. The last time I was in Athens, a couple of years earlier, we talked about her spending some time in Phoenix with my family. She was skeptical because of her health but her desire to see her grandchildren overpowered the handicap of the illness.

The next day as I saw my mother coming through the gate of the Phoenix Airport, I felt proud of her. It was an entirely different feeling than the one I had so many years ago when I was on that train. My heart was overflowing with love and pride that she was my mother. The way she looked at her grandchildren said it all; sometimes words are not necessary to describe feelings.

She stayed with us for three months. It was difficult for her because of the summer heat in Phoenix and the different lifestyle in this country. But not once did she complain. She was glad to spend time with my family.

I remember her spending time at my restaurant. She sat in her chair, knitting the entire time. I remember that she learned a few words of English. Despite the language handicap, she made more friends than I had. I was amazed at how she did that. She was a remarkable woman.

Nikos Ligidakis

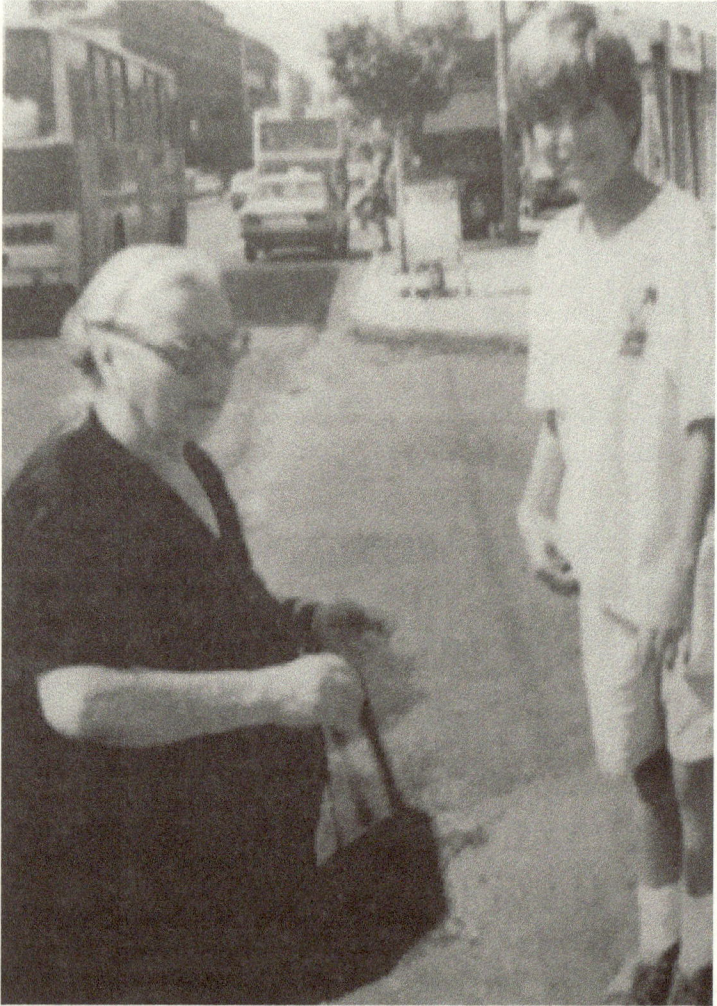

Mother with her grandson Steve in Athens

26

HEARTFELT

I looked around my restaurant. Nothing reminded me of days past. Hundreds of people gathered in the restaurant, not to have dinner or shop for desserts. They were helping with the preparation of meals. Others were bringing food donations or waiting to take food deliveries to those in need.

The menu offered this week was not the extensive, complicated menu served throughout the years, but a very simple one: roasted turkey with mashed potatoes, gravy, cranberry sauce, yams, and vegetables.

The atmosphere was tense yet brilliant. The phones rang constantly; people worked tirelessly; the energy was intoxicating. As the hours went by, mountains of foods were piling high.

I sat in a corner for a few minutes to marvel at the atmosphere. It had been almost sixty hours of non-stop preparing to give meals to the unfortunate. I was exhausted, but I didn't want to leave, I did not want to miss any of these moments.

Resting in the corner of the restaurant, I struggled to comprehend the events of the past hours. The thousands of volunteers, the hundreds of donors, it was impossible to count, impossible to remember.

Each year Thanksgiving came too soon. I anticipated

Thanksgiving like a great holiday every year. It was a celebration of the human spirit; a time to share hope.

I remembered that my parents had humble dreams and always did noble deeds. They never dreamed of becoming famous and legendary. They were wise, just, and courageous and because of that, in my eyes, they were the rulers of the universe. Because of that, I understood later in life that seeking fame, legacy, and material wealth just for recognition are human addictions.

I remember, when I was a bit older, asking my father if he ever had dreams of gaining wealth and living a more comfortable life. "Son," he said, "I have a great life. Besides the less we want, the more is available to others."

Since I was a little boy, I was fascinated with the beauty and the magnificence of the human spirit. My joy was to see people's greatness and I felt fortunate to walk on the same grounds where so much history was made.

My parents taught me in their gentle mannerism that all problems would be solved with patience and that I would reach a stage in my life that my dreams would be realistic. "Impossible is nothing – you are the only one that could choose the life you want. But, choose carefully." My father told me once.

On the night of Thanksgiving, the restaurant was quiet. It was the calm after the great storm. This was the year that we provided meals for thirty-two thousand needy citizens. To complete the project over five-thousand volunteers helped. Thousands of people donated food, and hundreds more delivered the meals to the homes and shelters. Somewhere around town thousands of people felt some hope to carry their spirits and hopes until tomorrow. But tomorrow darkness would again cover their hearts. Our efforts on every Thanksgiving were to deliver a bright sun into their misery, and a ray of hope for them knowing that some people cared. Hopefully, those unfortunate humans would realize that the world was not such a bad place and perhaps a better life was waiting for them.

At the end besides the great feelings, there was very little remaining food littering the tables in the restaurant. A few volunteers cleaned the kitchen. It was time for me to go. Tomorrow would start another hectic year in my restaurant.

My children came to visit me at home. They have grown so tall. Where did time has gone? I closed the door behind the children as they left. I looked around the house. I knew I had everything I wanted in life.

The years have gone by so quickly. My childhood seems like it was in another lifetime. Since then I discovered the worth of my heroes' deeds, those who silently, tirelessly revealed the answers about the purpose of life.

The years past were challenging, yet the rewarding feeling of doing something noble once in a while balanced the troubling moments.

Hard work was not a punishment but the way of life I have chosen.

It did not matter how many people noticed me walking by as long as the few who did were affected by my deeds.

My Heroes, My Town

27

LOVE REUNION

The news came suddenly via telephone. It was my sister, calling from Athens.

"Mother," she said over the telephone. Her voice was sober.

I sensed what had happened, but I had to ask. "What about Mother?"

There was not even a hesitation or a pause. "Her life has ended," she said.

"I am coming to Greece," I said.

"No, you do not have time," she said.

"I want to see her one last time."

"You are going to go through the same ordeal you went through with father," she reminded me.

Life has gone by so quickly. It was not that long ago that we were small children in Kiato. Mother was always there to care for us, and she was with us when we moved to Athens to go to school. She always acted the same when she saw us; her face would brighten with love. She did not like it when I was out playing soccer because she knew I was neglecting my homework. She embraced our friends with love and she fought for our rights. I saw her travel beyond the ocean and was fortunate to spend some time with her on my visits to Greece. I slowly discovered more of her inner strength; to deal with life's most difficult moments.

She had simple needs and reachable goals.

My mother had been ill for some time since the death of my father. Her health had slowly deteriorated. Maybe on the surface, she appeared strong throughout the years, but I know that inside the pain of losing the man she loved dearly was devastating. I guess it is true that when people lose their twin soul, a part of them dies as well.

For several years my mother went on frequent trips with a group of seniors. They traveled on the weekends by bus to several sites around the country. On a particular weekend, their bus was on its way back to Athens. It made a stop near my hometown of Kiato, for the travelers to get ice cream. My mother loved ice cream. Not just any kind, but the type that was homemade in that one store. She ate her ice cream and re-boarded the bus, joking with the other passengers as she usually did. She sat on her seat, exchanged a few words with the lady sitting next to her, then closed her eyes peacefully for her eternal rest.

It happened near the town where she was born and raised, among people she enjoyed, and with her favorite treat for her last bite. And it happened so peacefully. She was taken to a nearby hospital where she was pronounced dead.

The tears for my father have dried out and have turned into pleasant memories. But my mother still chokes me up when I think of her. She is one of the few people of whom a mere thought easily put a smile on my face. She inspires peace and exuberance in me.

My father's funeral was held in the small church of Panagia, in the middle of hundreds of pine trees, the same spot we went as children for picnics and on the same grounds where we played soccer.

My mother's funeral was held in Agia Sotira, the church across the street from my father's taverna.

I watched so many funerals from the taverna. At the passing of the funeral, everyone closed their doors for respect. I remember every time a funeral went by my father made us close the taverna's door, and we watched the passing from behind the glass of the door.

I looked at my watch. It was a very early morning where I was, but it was afternoon in Kiato where the funeral was taking place. I could see her passing by my school and in front of the taverna where she spent most of her life, past the butcher shop and the vegetable store where she shopped thousands of times, continuing down past the coffee shop where my father took his afternoon breaks and the bakery where we got fresh hot bread. I can still see her walking up and down the streets of Kiato greeting everyone on her way, chatting with friends.

This time, she was carried through the agora. The store from which she bought our school books was still there. The pastry shop whose pastries she loved was left behind also. Hundreds of people followed her, passing by the square, where we played as children, and then over the little bridge where, as a child, I planned the big trip with my two friends. Then they turned on the road to the cemetery. I imagined my three brothers and my cousin carrying her and wondered if they remembered to place my photograph by her heart as she had asked.

My father's funeral had come from the other side of town. He was carried past the railroad tracks and into the cemetery from the opposite direction of my mother's procession. Just as in life they came from different directions to meet in a union for the rest of their lives. Now their paths crossed once again, at the corner of the cemetery. Mother was placed to rest right next to father.

Finally, they were together again, this time for eternity. In my heart, there was satisfaction thinking of them together.

One year later I went to Greece for her memorial. I walked into the church of Agia Sotira for the first time after the remodeling was completed. The priest was one of my schoolmate's in grammar school, Father Apostolis. He knew my mother well since we were children. My uncle, Giorgos, was there, her only remaining brother, as were all the relatives and so many of their old friends. Even Mr. Katharios joined us and reminded me of the time long ago when he cut off the spear hooks stuck in my foot.

We went to my mother's grave for the service. Every one of the people who were on the bus when she passed away was there. In fact, they had leased the same bus and the same driver to bring them for the memorial.

I smiled, thinking that my mother would have liked that. She would have loved everyone there because her heart was a river of endless love.

Before I left their resting place, I visited the graves of my grandparents, my uncles, and my aunts. The afternoon mellow sunlight and the soft shadows of the thick cypress trees created a serene environment.

I glanced back to my parents' place of rest and smile; at last together again.

28

THE JUDGE

There was one part of the agora near my father's taverna which was a feast of the senses. There was the seductive aroma of melted chocolate and the pastry shop's dazzling showcase of cakes and pastries. Across the street, was the savory scent of deep-fried loukoumades; fried sweetened dough balls dipped in honey and cinnamon. On the opposite side the enticing smells of freshly baked bread coming out of the oven. There were roasted peanuts and brewed coffee. Blending into this euphoric surrounding was the savory array of aromas coming out of my father's taverna. The dominance of culinary purity is forever sealed in my psyche. Especially the honey and cinnamon aroma that woke us up; traditionally my mother would make loukoumades on our name days.

Between my mother and father, they raised a child with the divine calling of toothsome foods. Our dinner table was a place of community for our family. There was no fundamental principle used for our table setting, other than everyone was welcomed, and that there would be plenty of food. There would always be a conversation around the dinner table. The talks varied from stories of the past to current events or enlightening the curiosity of the young ones. The dinner time was a lengthy ritual of memorable tastes and words of wisdom. Besides the unforgettable flavors, there were some memorable moments, like the watermelon sharing. We all loved a cold, sweet watermelon in the summertime, especially the center part; the heart, as we called it. My dad would slice the watermelon and put the best part on his plate. Some of our friends who sat at our dinner table for the first time, they thought, "what is wrong with this man, taking the best part for himself." After the watermelon was sliced and served to everyone, our father counted the people sitting at the table and divided the heart of the watermelon into equal pieces.

I watched my father do this so many times with many other foods we all loved, and I was impressed at how justly he divided the best parts of the foods onto everyone's plate.

My father was the equivalent of democracy. There was no pretense with him; everything was straightforward. I believe that his straightforward approach earned him a lot of respect.

To become a great leader, one must cultivate the virtue of respect, to insist on worthy beliefs and actions. Growing up, respect was merited for our elders, especially to those who gained knowledge and wisdom through a disciplined lifestyle.

Our mother and grandmother were iconic images and our father was the just leader of our universe.

Sharing the heart of the watermelon might seem an insignificant gesture to many, but to a child, it translates to love and respect for equality. When dad cut the heart into equal pieces and divided it onto our plates, he was not concerned with how much we ate. He only wanted to make sure that the particular food we all loved was not going to cause divisions among his children. The justification of equal treatment of all became, in my young mind, the ultimate measure of respect for someone responsible for leading a group of people.

My Heroes, My Town

29

GIORGOS

Talking about respecting people; here is a story about my brother Giorgos.

My travels around the world brought me to Toronto, Canada. There I reconnected with one of my childhood friends. He had migrated to Toronto and now had a good job and a family with two children. After a short stay in Toronto, I found my way back to Chicago.

I spent my first years in Chicago trying to settle into this new culture.

It was a cold autumn evening. Darkness had fallen in the old neighborhood. The streets outside my window were misty and lonely.

I glanced behind me, to the past; there was my beautiful Greece in turmoil once again.

I looked ahead of me; there was America, unfamiliar and encouraging.

The phone rang. It was Giorgos.

"I am in Toronto," he said.

"How did you get there?" I asked.

"It's a long story. I need help to cross over."

He knew my friend well since we all grew up together. I gave

Giorgos the friend's number and asked him to contact him and stay with his family until we figure out what to do. Arrangements were made, but unfortunately, when he tried to cross over to the United States, he was taken by the immigration department.

Sleep escaped me the night before going to Detroit to pay his bail money to get him out. When I went in front of the judge to arrange the bail, the judge told me that I could not post bond for him. Before this incident, he had been in America. It was a time when Giorgos was with me for a while, but he could not adjust to this life and after a few years of working hard and being lonely, he went back to Greece. Unable to find a job there he decided to come back. And now he was sitting in a holding cell. My heart was broken, seeing him behind those iron bars, his face sad and confused.

He took the news with a good attitude saying, that was okay for him to go back, this was probably a mistake and it is for the best. I remember on my drive back to Chicago; I had one of my rare monologues with that higher being, the one I called master-crafter. The one who, supposedly, propelled me on this endless highway, driving on the snow-covered streets and the cold winds, surrounded by nothingness, by dark fields and gloomy skies.

Master crafter, you have taken away my blue sea, the whitewashed homes and the summer breeze. You have taken all I cherished and replaced the blue with the gray and the white with the black. And, if that wasn't enough, you are taking away my brother.

The hundreds of miles of the highway allowed me to reach the depth of my thoughts, trying to understand my worth and the reason of life's adversities. Long drives have always been my escape to realism, away from the cosmopolitan cities, apart from the pretenders and the treacherous, away from the stadiums, the companions, the dependent and the self-absorbed.

So, thank you, master crafter of the universe, you have forced me onto that lonely highway traveling alone, with my thoughts being my only companion. But now what?

I remember on my way home from the college I attended in Kallithea; I had to cross the metro station bridge, over the tracks. On my way down the stairs, there was my little brother, Giorgos, selling bananas out of a basket, already trying to help the family with extra income. He was always willing to work, always ready to help. When he was a little older, he worked in the famous Monastiraki flea market, where antique hunters search for treasures. One of my cousins owned one of those antique shops and hired Giorgos to restore old furniture. He worked hard and earned good money.

Giorgos always gave me money when I need it. He was never bitter; he gave from his heart. Most of his earning he gave to mother for household expenses.

As a teenager, he even saved enough money to buy a motorcycle. Because of his choice to work and help the family, he missed a lot of schooling. My older brother became a well-known watchmaker, designed his jewelry, and he was a unique troubleshooter mechanic to merchant marines. If there was trouble with the ship's engine that the regular crew could not fix, the ship owners would fly my brother to the destination to fix the problem. When it came to any mechanism, he knew it all.

My second brother was a lighthouse technician and continuously traveled to various Greek islands to maintain the lighthouses. He had a steady dream job and a secure retirement. I had my engineering degree, and my sister was determined to be a walking encyclopedia. Later on, she entered politics and opened her own business. But, Giorgos was a laborer. All he knew was hard work.

When my older brother got a call to fix an engine of a vessel going from Marseilles to Baltimore, he requested to take Giorgos with him.

My trip from Chicago to Baltimore to see them was a long drive. After dinner, Giorgos expressed his wish to stay and work in Chicago. It was his first time staying in America.

I was happy he was with me. He stayed for a few years and worked at various restaurants. Although, as always, a hard worker, he could not adjust to the lifestyle in America and decided to go back.

My little brother is nobody's fool. He is sharp, and he is kind. He holds no grudges against anyone. He envies no one and loves everyone. He is the personification of my mother. When back in Athens the second time he worked in my sister's business until he saved enough money to open his little business; a small neighborhood convenience store.

He met a nice girl, got married and had two beautiful daughters. Yes, it was for the best for him to go back.

A few years ago, when I visited him in Athens, he was waiting for me at the airport.

"Come on; I have a surprise for you," he said.

"What is it?"

"I'm not going to tell you."

After dropping my things in his home, he asked me to jump in the back of his motorbike. Then he reveals his surprise.

"I have two tickets for the Cup final soccer match," he said.

I smiled. He knows my passion for soccer, and those tickets

were a hot commodity. I sat in the back of his motorcycle, among a sea of cars and motorcycles, moving towards the Olympic Stadium. The vehicles were so close together that sometimes my knees touched them. The traffic lights and police officers tried desperately to keep traffic law and order. Giorgos rode, as did many others, between cars in danger of being squished.

Over sixty-thousand people moved towards the stadium, creating a pandemonium of songs, flags, and car horns. Yes, this is my Athens.

At the kick-off, the stands erupted and for ninety minutes, the noise was deafening. I watched Giorgos and I smiled because he seemed happy. Athens is where he belongs.

Giorgos is the nicest and the sincerest person I know. He projects kindness and love from every fiber of his being.

When our family visited Greece a few years back, on the few days we stayed in Athens, we visited his little shop often and everyone always left with bags full of goodies. My grandkids fell in love with my little, big brother and every time we mention a trip back to Greece; they get excited to go back and see "Uncle George."

This is my little brother; one of my heroes.

Giorgos in his little shop in Kallithea

Uncle George with his niece Lisa

30

EPIPHANY

I remember the first time I tried to talk to God. It was shortly after the death of my father. Before starting my conversation with God, I wasn't sure what to expect; a body or a spirit. As I began to talk, all that rolled into my imagination was an enormous face. The eyes of that face were the dominant feature; they seemed to overshadow the entire universe.

The impression that face took was an infinite command over my senses and I felt this image was the reflection of the absolute ruler of the universe. My first question was to ask for a favor but, it is not wise to ask favors from someone you just met. So, I introduced myself. I spoke for a while about my feelings and questioned the injustices that go on down here on earth; like the death of my father. And, once I thought I was on God's good side, I asked for my favor; to bring my father back and take me. It was an even trade to keep the universal balance – a life for a life.

After the death of my father, all I could think about was unfairness and a plethora of question about the reasoning of early death. You know, why he couldn't enjoy life with his children and grandchildren, following his retirement, and after working so hard throughout his life. So, I asked that powerful image to make it right. I thought that was fair enough.

I know that my request was foolish and done in a desperate moment. Bringing back the dead is scientifically impossible and beyond logic.

The mysteries of the universe have always fascinated me and tortured my existence. Often, I want to stop defining things, to rest my brains but I cannot help myself – I am addicted. I am confident that this powerful image adds to my fascination. The overwhelming energy of that image has doubled my perplexity about mysteries. It has gone to the torture chamber of my brains where I keep all the unanswered questions.

I admit that this image reminds me of my father's face, especially the eyes.

I believe my father's image manifested into my imagination to materialize that optical illusion. Of course, my request for exchanging life was foolish and selfish. My father would never have agreed to such a trade.

The peculiar thing about this experience was that it intrigued my curiosity about logic and the supernatural. Could those two poles coexist? I mean, could someone be a fan of both the New York Yankees and the Boston Red Sox? It is possible, I supposed. Or ideologically belong to both the extreme left and the extreme right? Now that is not possible; it is an oxymoron. And so it is improbable to find real answers in theology and the supernatural when one believes in logic and science.

I am certain that the death of my parents has changed my way of thinking. Those defining moments contributed to my intellectual growth, to entirely see the positive in the most tragic events. As a young man, I lived a carefree life. My commitment wasn't for anything and my responsibility was to no one.

Eventually, I had to choose between substance and emptiness.

As far as I remembered, there was always this intenseness in me that kept me in oblivion between a child's mind and an adult's responsibility. Slowly I began to find the clarity of my convictions. My parents were merely the catalysts molding my identity. Eventually, the choice between love and hate was clear. I feel more comfortable to identify wisdom and humility in the universal laws, without discarding someone else's beliefs and ideologies. I think that is realistic to seek love and harmony through logic. The theory of reasoning has clarified, for me anyway, the dilemma between philosophy and theology.

I often paraphrase life's advancement to a giant puzzle. At first, some odd pieces piled up. Separating them at first is difficult, but as you begin to identify the colors and shapes, it becomes easier to assemble it. It is a fact that the philosophy of one person is pure speculation.

Therefore, in philosophy, there are plenty of tragic thinkers, and so are the prophets in religion as well.

I can only follow a familiar path of logic on how to live a just life. I am not sure why seeking answers through logic is controversial for those who believe that heaven and hell is a place somewhere in the universe.

Should theology triumph over knowledge?

I don't get it why the views of sex, atheism, evolution, homosexuality, and abortion should fabricate a bridge to hell.

Why are there so many bitter conflicts of science versus faith? After all, it is facts versus speculation!

I believe that those who treat religion with extreme measure are disrespectful to God, because, they underestimate God by thinking that He is not beyond their pettiness and their envy.

After all, they are telling us that God is kind and loving.

I remember one day after a hard day's work. I was laying on my bed with my eyes closed. I imagined myself in the desert where it was hot, and I was lost. Suddenly that overwhelming image came back. It was not as vivid as it was the first time I saw it. This time, there was a hand. The palm lifted me up. I felt like an ant walking on a giant palm frond. It was moist after the day's rain. The moistness entered my mind and penetrated my senses. I felt the kindness of the image and it provided me with a shadow to protect me from the sun. The breath from the face was a breeze of fresh air, which gently cooled my body. It was an amazing feeling.

There are several passages throughout the bible that refer to God as a human form, and in other passages as just a spirit. Who knows for sure? All I know is that I saw my father's reflection in that enormous face; call it the face of God if you will.

Nikos Ligidakis

My dad with his friends celebrating life.

31

ANGUISH AND ELATION

Sitting on my brother's balcony in Athens, I reminisced about the days of long ago. It had been a while since I was back in Greece. Every time I am here, every time I breathe this air, I promise myself to come back frequently. I often wonder – how is it possible to stay away from a place that I am so bonded with?

It is four o'clock in the morning; the balcony is how I remember it, full of plants, herbs and flowers. It reminded me of when we were children in Kiato during the springtime walking by the home gardens and through the fields full of poppies, anemones and violets.

The air of Greece has drugged me once again.

Here is where my mind isolates the boisterous world and draws me into the magical universe of writing. The golden, mellow sunrise found me with endless handwritten pages. The urge to travel overcame me once again. I wanted to take a trip back to those places that had marked the journey of my life. As I drove away from my brother's home the morning was cloudy and a meager sun was laboring through the grey clouds.

My mind traveled back to my youth and how exciting it was to ride our bikes with friends to nearby cities. My friend Kostas the boy that was killed in one of the outings was a part of our riding gang. We rented our bicycles from Klis Bike Shop and on we went. We rode for endless hours visiting places of interest outside Kiato. One of our favorite destinations was the town of Xylokastro. It was a bit further than the usual places we visited, but it was worth the ride. Kostas had many relatives there since his family lived in Xylokastro before moving to Kiato. His parents moved back to Xylokastro for their retirement. One of my uncles had moved there as well.

I had the urge to visit Xylokastro. By late morning I was pulling into a town that was still beautiful yet somewhat unfamiliar. There were hundreds of swimmers in the clear blue waters of the sea and the densely wooded area at the edge of the city called Pefkias was overflowing with tourists and campers. I drove by Pefkias to reach the town's cemetery.

I searched for my childhood friend Kostas. His gravestone was covered with wild grass and the marble top had turned yellow from the passing of time. His parents were lying next to him. I cleaned out the wild grass and lit his candle.

I sat by their graveside and reminisced the time, a few years back, when I visited his parents. They always told me that my visits reminded them of happier times and that they felt the presence of their son when I was with them. The last time I was in their small home, it was winter. The father was lying in his death bed, the reflection of the raging burning wood in the fireplace was flickering some color on his pale face. The mother fed him some soup and then she sat by the fire. I felt his weak grip on my hand. "Thank you for coming." His voice, meager and colorless, penetrated my heart. The shock of their boy's death caused profound grief for both parents.

Kostas' father, the tall, strong man that I knew as a child was now reduced to bones and pale flesh. Life was leaving him. I held his hand.

I felt his broken heart shattering my body. Tears, in his eyes. Tears, in my eyes.

He lifted his head, looking directly into my eyes, and said, "I can't fight this pain anymore." He paused for a moment to take a deep breath. "I must rest now," he said quietly. I placed his hand gently by his side.

His wife, knitting by the fireplace, "for the grandchildren," she said.

When I was a child, I watched her walk on the streets of Kiato. She had an impressive figure, like the Italian movie stars. As I grew older, I understood why men turned their heads to marveled at her lingering walk, her beautiful olive eyes and her dark hair resting on her shoulders.

Now, she was sitting by the fire, dressed in black. Her hair was covered with a black kerchief. Her beautiful olive eyes had dried out from the pain and tears.

As I was getting ready to leave, she stood up and hugged me gently. I felt her pain surging through my arms and into my heart.

"Courage," I said. "Thank you for coming to visit us," she said. Outside the air was fragrant and the breeze crisp, but in my nostrils, there was the smell of medicine and the breath of death. As I walked away from the small house, the father's painful voice was ringing in my ears and the mother's saddened eyes were piercing my heart. I left the cemetery and drove towards the mountains. Multitudes of colored flowers emerged in home yards and decorated the balconies. Out on the fields, the trees were in full blossom. It was the beginning of the spring, a time when the bees labored from flower to flower, to prepare honey.

Approaching the mountains, I reached the narrow, winding road on the foot of the mountain. The continuing sharp, tight turns kept my focus on the road; I could only take a few brief glances below. The land beneath me had opened wide, decorated with acres of grapevines, windflowers and boundless trees. Climbing the mountain, I passed a few homes along the way and when I was almost to the top, I pulled into the little yard of a familiar house. It was a house that I had often visited in the past.

My aunt and uncle's home was small and simple. When I walked into their house, my aunt was surprised to see me. It had been I while since my last visit. My uncle walked in shortly after. He was just as I remembered him - animated. I think his character is what my father admired and every time he saw my uncle, dad's face brightened. This one uncle was closer to my dad than any of mother's other brothers.

After the welcoming hugs, I asked my uncle to tell me more about my father. He smiled as if he was saying, not right now. A few minutes later he got up from his chair.

"Come on. I'll tell you all about your father later." He wrapped his arm around me and walked to his car. After about a half an hour drive up the mountain, we stopped at a small village. A few tables were outside the small coffee shop standing at the edge of the mountain, overlooking the plains below. We sat on one of the tables.

My uncle joked around with the people sitting at the other tables. Then he turned to me and started talking. "I was the first of the family to meet your father when he visited Kiato from his military base. I encouraged your father to talk to your mother." He glanced beyond the mountaintop, his eyes longing of times past. "Those were difficult years my son. We survived hard times and we made the best with what we had." His voice softened remembering the years of youth. I had never seen that side of him before. I let him be with his thoughts. "Your father was some man. You do not find people like him often. He appeared in Kiato out of nowhere. Nobody knew where he came from. He spoke very little about himself. Kiato back then was not like now. Everyone who lived there was like a family and a stranger was spotted like a fly in milk. Now there are so many people; I don't even recognize most of them."

Then he went on to tell me how everyone disapproved of my father marrying my mother. "I stood by your father. I knew he was a good man. Next, it was your grandmother that warmed up to your father. And that was it. Once your grandmother welcomed your father the rest of the family came aboard." He paused for a while looking down at the breathtaking land. "You know, when I was young, I was a tough guy. I could stand on my own. But your father was the strongest man I knew." A smile appeared on his face. "Nobody messed with your father. He always came to protect me when I needed him."

"What about mother," I asked. "All you need to know about your mother is that she was the most beautiful girl," he said as he got up from his chair.

"Let's get something for dinner," he said. We walked toward the butcher shop. I was over fifty-years-old at that time and my uncle treated me with respect but also as a child that was under his protection.

"What kind of meat do you want today?" asked the short, heavy-set man with the white apron, sitting by his butcher block. Those two talked for a few minutes, then my uncle turned to me and said "Your father used the best meat and best foods. He taught me how to shop." Walking back to the car he said, "Don't forget, if it weren't for me bringing your father into the family, you wouldn't be around." We both had a good laugh.

Back home and during dinner, my uncle and aunt acted like newlyweds – at their old age they were still much in love.

My sleep was peaceful that night. In the morning we all sat outside in the small yard having coffee. The sun was climbing in the sky trying to erase the mist that covered the mountain.

"Come on, let's go and pick some vegetables," my uncle said.

Despite his age, he went down to the field below the house with a youthful walk. I followed him. Within a few minutes, I found myself among fruit trees. As we walked farther, there was a vegetable garden. He tried to decide between zucchini and eggplant. "What do you want for lunch?" he asked.

"I don't know, whatever you think," I said. And there were green beans, tomatoes, cucumbers, peppers and all kinds of herbs. He filled his basket with vegetables and walked up to the house. Seeing my uncle picking vegetables with such vigor, I wondered if it was his humor and laughter is that kept him young.

This seemed a world far removed from the one I lived the last few decades. The beauty of the surrounding nature was overwhelming. My mood was in direct contrast from a couple of days ago when I visit my young friend in the cemetery.

After lunch, I thanked them for their hospitality.

"Stay for a few days. God knows when we will see you again," my aunt said.

"I am sorry, but I have to go," I told her.

The hectic life of the world was calling me back. As I was driving down the mountain to face the boisterous world, I felt privileged that at least for a couple of days I was on top of the mountain.

The despair of grieving parents I visited long ago, and joyfulness extended into the older age was separated just by a few kilometers.

My Heroes, My Town

32

LAND OF LEGENDS

I left Xylokastro and headed for Sparta. Even now, after a lifetime of absence, my heart throbs with happiness and pride when I drive through the mountains and the villages when I see the coastlines and the islands.

As I drove deeper into the country, I gradually felt that I was touching something abstract, something unbroken. All around me there was undeniable strength and absolute grace; the two elements that keep the land of Greece forever enticing.

I passed through rugged regions, and enchanting valleys - harshness and tenderness standing side-by-side, coupling like a man and a woman.

No matter where I went, I found divine traces. I felt the spirit of my ancestors; heroes who have passed over the myths to create a land of enduring spirit.

Mountains towered around me. From their peaks, resolute warriors ran into the battlefields, driven by the ruthless command that defines the duty of man into life in war; do not laugh, do not talk, your sole purpose in life is to win.

Stretched out below the mountains were the fruited plains; this is Sparta, the land that is associated with the ultimate warriors; The Spartans. I passed through valleys where great battles had taken place in the past and coastline where thousands of battleships had sailed.

I drove on for a while and stopped on the countryside to walk on the land that Homer immortalized. The soil was fragrant, the dewdrops hanging from the citrus trees. A gentle breeze blew and filled my heart with refreshing dew.

I felt high energy surrounding me. Maybe it was the breath of Homer, who with his pen transformed the strength of men and the beauty of a woman into immortality in the classics, the Iliad and the Odyssey.

It is to Homer to whom this small land owes its eternal glory. Without the genius of the poet, this land, these names, would have passed in history unrecognizable, like so many brave warriors, like so many beautiful women who have made their passage across time and perished. It is the story that has also become a love cry, a cry that traverses the centuries and awakens man's yearning for tenderness and the woman's need for strength. Driving along, I found myself in the sacred hill of Mystra, the heart and soul of Byzantine movement. I walked through narrow, twisting streets surrounded with lemon and orange orchards and cypress groves. Beyond the green paradise was a treeless land, studded with charming Byzantine churches.

It was here, in Peloponnese, where the Franks, encased in armor, galloped in as conquerors, but beautiful Greek women, with olive skin, raven black hair and large black eyes, conquered the hearts of the fierce warriors. It was then that the victors were vanquished in Greek blood, and tenderness and strength bonded once again.

My appetite for the land of Greece was not yet satisfied as I felt the urge to visit more places. I found a place to rest for the night.

The sunlight began to shine in the beautiful city beneath. It was the dawn of Sunday, the church bells echoed through the city, calling the faithful to come and pray.

Beneath my balcony unfolded one of my most beloved cities, the city of Nafplio. A city with modern-era neoclassical buildings, integrated with homes of traditional architectural style, partly influenced by the Venetians.

The sea was calm and turquoise blue. Further into the sea emerged the fortified island that protected the harbor of the city during the numerous invasions throughout the centuries.

As I left Nafplio and passed the ancient Corinth, I headed for Epidavros, home of the old amphitheater and the ancient sanctuary of Asclepius. According to the legend, Asclepius was the son of Apollo and Coronis. His sanctuary was the largest healing center in antiquity. Asclepius' symbol was the serpent, an animal that lives above and within the earth, therefore being familiar with both worlds and communicating with living organisms in mysterious ways. Traveling through the land that witnessed so many struggles and so much joy, I understood the immense importance of this unique country. It was here that the destiny of humankind was at stake. It was here when the barbaric waves of men, clenched with inhumanity, arrived and were defeated by the human nobility.

During that trip to Greece, I felt the rhythm that has governed the life here since ancient times. There were ancient ruins and statues thousands of years old that seemed to come alive. It was when the art was born with passion and expression.

In the Asclepion sanctuary, the sick people would go through a ritual cleansing and spend the night isolated in the sleeping ward. The gods would appear in their dreams and suggest the treatment they should follow. Not excluding surgery and drug treatment, therapy of the Asclepion relies on the patient's shattering their physical experience with the supernatural, an experiment that must have given immediate and impressive results.

Epidavros is known mainly for its amphitheater. It is the most celebrated in the ancient world and famous for its perfect acoustics.

Epidavros' center stage is also a sacred place to the modern Greeks. In January of 1822, it was here, after four hundred years of Turkish oppression, that Greek independence was announced and the flag of Greece was raised, once again, by free hands.

On my way to Olympia, I drove by villages etched on the green slopes of the hills. I stopped and spoke with kind-hearted peasants, people who knew that simplicity was the antidote to greed and stress.

Walking around the ruins of Olympia, I realized that no other people in history understood the real value of sports. The Greeks knew that civilization begins the moment that we satisfy our essential needs. One of those needs is to enjoy leisure.

I stood amidst the colossal stones that were smashed by earthquakes and destroyed by barbarians and Christians alike.

Sadness overcame me as I thought of how many pieces of art were burned and looted by the numerous invaders throughout the centuries. Olympia is where the gods competed long before men did. It was there where Zeus fought Cronos, and where Apollo defeated Hermes in the running.

For the Greeks, gymnastics was a required preparation. Harmony of the body and the mind was their supreme ideal. Hercules, the great hero, was their supreme example.

Strolling through the museum of Olympia, I marveled at

the fascinating figures of Hermes, Nike and Apollo, statues that artists have brought to life with clever hands and creative eyes.

It is true that when passiveness reigns over our lives that artistic passion declines. It is then when we arrive into a voiceless era, devoid of extraordinary ideas, a time we sink back into darkness.

I found my way to Delphi and stood on the top of the mountain, a place between heaven and earth. I glanced beyond the mountain, surrounded by hills and ravines, and wondered why the ancients chose this place to build the Oracle and how was it possible to create a city of marble on top of this steep mountain.

On the highest point, there was the stadium where the first music and poetry competitions in history took place. Green trees and clear light surrounded it. There I realized another factor that charms the Greek earth; it is the glow of history.

It is in this land, soaked with success and failure, that the cry of freedom and democracy is bound with memory.

We live in a time when powerful forces rise from the east and the west, a time that our responsibility for freedom and democracy seems to be more critical than ever. The two monstrous impulses, the west and the east, must find a solution, a synthesis of reasoning to end their rivalry of arrogance and power.

When I was a young man, I thought that the core of my existence and survival was about strength. "Be strong and you could survive anything in life," I often heard from people around me. Later in life, I realized that I must drop this egocentric attitude and adopt tenderness to balance my rebellious self.

My Heroes, My Town

33

THE BEARS

The moon was playful that evening. It was jumping from cloud to cloud against a sky brushed with shades of gray and blue. The misty evening sky had turned gloomy as the darkness of the night covered the island. Thunder rolled down from the sky and the lightning blazed to expose the obscure images around me. Out of the darkness appeared the turquoise sea and stucco houses in vibrant pastels: blue, orange, mauve and yellow. The blazing sky unveiled silver-green olive groves, citrus trees, and there were large and small fishing boats rocking on the immense sea.

As I was walking through the streets of Kerkyra, a light rain began to fall. It was my last evening there before returning to my hometown and then back to America. At that moment I felt that I belonged to neither world, trapped between human tragedy and human laughter. As the rain intensified a bit, I slowed down my walk. I closed my eyes and lifted my face to feel the rain. A colorful giddiness as sweet and tender like a morning mist captivated my mind. Behind the mist, I observed a world half stable, half composed of illusions.

Not too long ago I was a curious child. Now my heart was a dark unyielding mystery; after all the lessons, I remained inquisitive. Ahead of me was the direction in which the merciless voice of the past kept urging me to move, to keep searching.

The crowded cafes and noisy tavernas were quiet by now, the storefronts were dark and the thousands of people who frequented the agora had gone home.

Past midnight, I walked up the marble steps of the old hotel. Sleep quickly came over me. It was then that the bears appeared! The bears were enormous; they seemed angry and dangerous. They gathered on the side of the hill. I had never seen such greenery. There were trees and bushes laden with bright green leaves. The earth was covered with thick grass and embroidered with yellow, red and white flowers spreading all the way up to the hills. It was on one of those hills from where the roar of the bears disturbed the morning silence. Suddenly, the bears began to walk towards the forest where I was hiding.

I raised my rifle and aimed at them. Through the gun's telescope, their eyes appeared angry, yearning for human flesh.

Slowly the bears stepped towards me; I felt my life threatened; it was them or me.

I aimed at them and started to squeeze the trigger of my rifle, anxious to defend my space.

"I can't... I can't shoot," I shouted.

I threw my rifle on the ground and its trigger went off. The fire then discharged from the barrel of the gun creating an awful sound. It hurt my ears and blinded my eyes. The green image of the earth vanished into flames and smoke.

The bears were startled and retreated a few steps. They seemed frightened, but only for a moment. I counted six of them.

Suddenly, they seemed infuriated. They roared and retraced their steps toward me.

Their roars echoed throughout the land.

I looked around. The faces of my three brothers appeared from behind the greenery.

They stood to my left, and to my right.

"Don't worry, brother, we'll protect you," they said with one voice.

The bears were closing in fast. My brothers raised their guns.

"Pick up your gun. You've got to shoot," my older brother shouted at me.

The bears were a few feet away. They stood on their back feet and towered high in front of me. Their black fur covered the green background of the earth.

I looked up into the face of the bear closest to me. I saw long sharp teeth, a foamy mouth and angry red eyes.

Two enormous paws with long, sharp nails wrapped around me. Thunderous gunshots startled me; the sounds came from my left, and from my right. I opened my eyes.

Beyond my window, the moon had veered away from the clouds, its soft light was reflecting on the calm seawaters. Through the glass door of my room, I observed the island in calmness, not a bear anywhere in sight.

The rising sun brought the activity back to the streets. Leaning from my window I looked at men, women, bicycles, and storefronts opening their doors to display fruits and fish. I interpreted the last night's dream with my recent military experience.

I walked on the small streets of the island; I smiled, thinking that by the end of the day all these things will be dispersed into emptiness, all will scatter under the gentle night sea breeze to make room for the nightlife.

The salty breeze of the island reminded me of precious

memories of yesteryears: our house by the beach, the school by the sea, the small port with the fishing boats, blue sea, and calm waves.

Seabirds flew beneath the blue sky, periodically attacking the surface of the sea, searching for food. Colorful fishing boats lingered on the gentle waves. The fishermen were coming on shore, bringing in their catch. People gathered on the pier to shop for fish.

Decades later I was back on the beautiful island and I was reminded of that dream, when I visited the island after I was released from the military; the element of strength was the cornerstone of my existence back then. However, the second time I visited the island my perspective had changed; tenderness had now entered in my heart. It was now that could see the beauty of the island that I had missed during the thunder and lightning.

34

FRIENDS

Driving on the Los Angeles highways, I wondered who called this the City of Angels? How was it possible for angels to survive in this chaos, the civil hostility and the gloomy smog?

I glanced at the endless lines of cars - everything was moving so slow. I saw people with angry faces, talking to themselves and making offensive gestures.

I thought about my journey from my quiet hometown of Kiato, to this deafening noise of car horns and engines. I thought about that single event in the army that inaugurated the trip of my life's transformation. It had been an amusing adventure traveling around the world. I have seen strange lifestyles, faced many adversities and learned so many lessons.

On the outskirts of this city, on the port of San Pedro, long ago, as we were getting ready to sail to Japan, there were three new crewmen who joined the ship. One of them was Tolis, a friend while growing up in Athens. For the next year or so, we worked on deferent vessels together. Our plan was to earn money and disembark on a country where we would like to stay for a while and explore their culture. We served together in four vessels.

The first place we disembarked in Bremerhaven in Germany. We took the train to Hamburg and when we arrived there, it was late at night. We had no idea where to find a place to spend the night. Tired of looking, we found a park with full-grown trees, thick green foliage and decided to rest on the benches. The sky above was adorned with myriads of stars. Phantasmagoric lights ascended from the ground and climbed up to the dark-blue sky. The moon was nearly round and bright yellow but soon the blackness was absolute; exhaustion overtook my senses. I felt the cold air penetrating my bones and an involuntary shiver overwhelmed my entire body. I opened my eyes to see the muted colors of pinks and yellows emerging on the eastern sky. Tolis was laying on another bench; his body folded trying to protect himself from the morning's chill.

After the sun came up, we found a hostel to stay in. The young people staying in the hostel suggested visiting this one entertaining area. At first, I wasn't sure that was where I wanted to be. The area was full of striptease clubs and rowdy bars. We were getting ready to leave this area when we noticed groups of young people entering a place called the Star Club. The club hosted unknown rock bands that mostly played hits from other artists. That night there was a group called the Beatles who did play other hits but also some original music. Little we knew we were witnessing history.

Next was the sunny Puerto La Cruz in Venezuela. A city with beautiful white-sand beaches, the best corn flour empanadas, and a plethora of open-air clubs from where the loud sounds of Merengue and Joropo blasted everywhere. I've watched my friend Tolis get in between the hundreds of dancers lingering to the rhythmic music. He was in his element.

Then back to Europe, in Marseilles. From there we took the train to Paris, where we endured endless hours of walking. We walked past bridges, churches, chestnut trees and soot-covered buildings. We strolled among the thousands of people walking the streets where there were music and bicycles, outdoor cafes and newspaper kiosks; a city with a charming, playful face.

It was on the heels of the winter; an impassive sun seemed composed of mist, melancholy and inexpressible tenderness. We walked around the corner from Bibliotheque Nationale, a few blocks from the river Seine, the Eiffel Tower and Notre Dame Cathedral. The intoxication of Paris lasted several days.

The crowded streets, the theaters, the museums, the Gothic churches, the artists stroking their brushes on canvas, the Sunday football fever, all whirled around our hearts until the drunkenness of Paris wore off. The world steadied and grew stable. It was a sign for us that it was time to move on. We found a vessel from Marseilles and a month later we were out of Paris and on to New Orleans. We stopped by the French Quarter for a bite to eat. The city by the port was alive with people laughing and singing and dancing. From there I decided that it was time for me to go back and serve my military duty. Tolis wanted to move on, to find his Ithaca.

I smiled at the thought that his spirit had remained untamed and his young heart yearned for more adventures. But mine was settling – that was not the life I wanted.

"I am moving on," he said, "I want to see the world."

I looked at him and smiled, "Good-by my friend." He was only twenty years old.

"One of these days I want to stay in Japan, finding me a nice girl, get married and start a family." he had told me once. He was on his way to Japan when the vessel he was on, sank and buried him in its watery grave.

Driving amidst the pandemonium of cars on the Los Angeles freeways I was reminded of those days long ago. Shortly, I noticed familiar places around me; ships were floating on the water and other vessels docked by the shipyards. I was driving on a long bridge, heading towards San Pedro.

As the mellow afternoon sun was tilting in the western horizon, I found myself on the pier in San Pedro. The shops on the pier were busy with customers; fishermen were trying to sell their daily bounty. Boats and yachts were lingering on the gentle sea waves. It was familiar scenery, yet so distant.

Where I grew up we were surrounded with beautiful sunsets, shops by the beach-front, fishermen coming out from the sea, and boats floating on blue waters.

Here, the colors were different from what I was used to, the faces unfamiliar, the shops unrecognizable, and the fishermen were not thick-skinned old men whose bodies were soaked with sun and salt.

I parked my car overlooking the endless ocean. A melancholic voice emerged from the radio, "…sitting on the dock of the bay…"

From the dock, I observed that mystical body of water, a place that hides myriads of secrets. A watery grave of millions of people lost in the sea, among them my friend Tolis, a modern Odysseus, who journeyed the world seeking his Ithaca but finding Cyclops and Sirens instead. I missed my friend; I missed his optimism and his vigor. My beloved sea had swallowed him. How ironic!

"I'm sitting on the dock of the bay, watching' the tide, roll away…" the voice continued to sing, nostalgic and lamenting.

A few teardrops rolled from my eyes. It is not possible that

I should feel sadness after such a rich life, full of adventures and lessons? But I did.

I guess I had yet to bring into harmony all the issues that wrestled inside of me.

At this moment I felt angry, revengeful and unforgiving.

Since I was a little boy watching the funeral procession from behind the taverna's glass door, the death of people whom I knew has always depressed me. "…sitting on the dock of the bay, wasting time…" I had no time to waste; I had to deal with the issues that wrestled inside me.

From my pocket, I pulled out the half of a silver dollar, an item that I was carrying with me since the days of my world travels. Along the way of our travels, Tolis cut a silver dollar in half, in a zigzag pattern. He handed me the one half. "Friends forever for hope and strength," he had told me.

I held it in my fist. The sun was laying itself down to a well-deserved rest; its work was done for the day. The night was about to spread its darkness on the endless body of water in front of me. I raised my arm and threw my half of the silver dollar into the sea, as far as I could.

I sent it out to find the other half, buried in that mysterious grave we call the sea.

"Goodbye, my friend."

I left San Pedro and drove towards Phoenix, a godforsaken land, a place without shops on the pier, without boats lingering on the gentle waves, without sun-soaked fishermen, a place of a different beauty, one that I have grown to love. It was a place I called home, the home of my children.

My Heroes, My Town

35

DISTANT WORLDS

Heavy pellets of hail were falling outside my home. In Greece, the mountains and the beaches would have gleamed in the morning sun, but here, the light, which had crept over the muddy yard it was pale and unpleasant. There was not a single person on the streets. The world seemed lifeless and callous. Eventually, the hail reduced into the rain. A mystic empathy awakened inside of me. Between the rainfall and beyond the murk I envisioned my father's face and heard my mother's laughter. A range of emotions began to orbit inside my mind as the memories carried me to the adventures of the past; times that infiltrate my subconscious mind periodically, like a ghost clinging, irresistible and stubborn. An array of emotions kept surfacing, even when I tried to defend my sanity with logic or cynicism. These emotions bring along unpleasant images; the military ordeal, my first fight, suffering, hate, hunger or injustice. It brought along images of loss of the loved ones. Death has always been something unbearable for me; I cannot deal with it. I am thinking what I could have done differently to prevent the mistakes I have made along the way. I have this problem; I blame myself when things go wrong – I must stop doing that. But how can one forget the pretentious smiling faces, superficial handshakes and slimy kisses.

How is it possible to watch people laugh and drink and dance in apathy and silliness?

How can I laugh, drink and dance?

I have not yet managed to be completely free from the ghost nested in my conscience.

I realize that great things have happened since then, events that make my tormenting issues seem insignificant.

Someone told me once that if you write and speak about poverty, oppression and wickedness, you transform pain into beauty and it is only then that pain departs from your consciousness. I am trying to remember who told me that, because I want to respond, to say that I have seen, with my own two eyes, warriors with kindness and indomitable will, hurt but moved on and lived productive lives.

I want to tell that person that nothing leaves our consciousness, but it is possible to transform pain into beauty; the pain is necessary to remind but not to dwell. Obliviousness does not erase the pain. The rain is hitting hard on the glass; the world beyond my window is composed of water and mud. How wonderful it would be to use the mud to mold a new world, a place in which we can all laugh and drink and dance.

The world as I desire does not exist. Will it ever?

My inner voice is tells me that even though the world I crave does not exist, it should exist because I want it to exist. This is an idea that has thrown me into turmoil.

What a fearful responsibility it is, for those who care, to bear the world's injustice and contempt. It is when I found my escape in a pen and a paper that I was able to clarify my thoughts and formulate my true feelings.

The years have gone by so quickly and the societal changes

are so visible.

The future looks bright; maybe there is a cure for the illness and the hunger.

At least an aura of spring is finally coming to replace the torrential rain that still pounds outside my window.

I always had the urge to approach life's victories and downfalls philosophically. I refused to become a misanthropist. But, to become a philosopher, one must manage to bring peace to the issues that have torn the heart apart.

I spend endless nights reading and writing in solitude, to allow knowledge to move into my unrecognizable soul and to fill my heart with human sorrow.

To change ourselves, and the world around us, we must forever be like the teenager who is searching for answers. Knowledge is an eternal fire, which burns inside each one of us, a fire that diminishes as we become more analytical.

But, for now, I must watch the rain that turns the earth to muddy waters again.

By early morning, the rain stopped and the sun was up. It was a usual hot day in Phoenix, the thirsty earth had dried up and the temperature reached triple digits. By the afternoon the torrid air was motionless, and the sun pitied no one; its rays blazing down determined to burn every living creature.

The cemetery I entered was a little different than the one in Kiato. The headstones and the crosses lined up in a casual landscape, adorned by few trees, shading a bit of relief on the burning land.

I stopped by her graveside. Her image mounted slowly in my mind.

I thought of the perplexed emotions that accompany the loss

of a loved one. It is a progression of feeling that moves and shifts to unknown emotions and ends when it inflicts the heart with tremendous pain. Her image appeared, as I first knew her; her lively green eyes, her long black hair and her youthful smile.

I smiled thinking that she was the only one who indeed knew the first few miles of my life's journey here in America. The difficult years, when I was a lost soul, trying to find my way into this new and strange culture.

It was a time that nothing made sense. It felt as if I was thrown into an arena with warriors who carried weapons unknown to me. I stood among them barren and confused. And, I had left behind all my tools: my language, my education, my family, my customs, my holidays, and all I was carrying with me was the audacity to believe in myself.

Behind me stood the dictators, waiting with their raised swords, ready to slice the necks of those who opposed them. Ahead of me was an endless land inhibited by multi-ethnic people, a society flourishing from foreign seeds and divided into a multitude of religions.

I sat on the ground to think. What an extraordinary journey this has been!

I would not have been able to carry on this journey without the precious gifts she left for me; our children and grandchildren.

In the days of our youth, there were cultural attitudes and a different approach to lifestyle. I was the seeker, the adventuring spirit; she was content, satisfied with her cultural environment. Two opposite, antagonistic energies.

I came to confess to her that youth is a restless beast, one that only the passage of time can tame and turn into a gentle soul.

I left the cemetery thinking of how much she helped me

break the barriers of traditions and find solace in judgment. And, through our children, I was able to bridge my world with hers.

It was much later, in one of my trips to the northwest, that I saw this new country's spectacular beauty. My companion in life and her family crossed to Victoria, Canada, where I was amazed at people's kindness and the beauty of the colorful flowers and the majestic trees.

We ended up in Oregon, new to her extended family and where just about every member of the family had gathered to celebrate the Fourth of July.

Growing up in Athens, I went to discos and parties with my friends. I grew up listening to foreign music and watched foreign films because that was the cool thing to do.

We knew all that was happening in the world.

We argued about politics and idealism because we were young, and we knew everything.

We tried to be stylish and different. We were boisterous and angry and stubborn and authorities on all subjects, again, because we were young, and we knew it all. But, I was never comfortable with all of these. I have always been a stranger to ephemeral joys since I was a young man - I have always felt that way.

Youth is a monster with unlimited energy and strength, but it does not know it.

The mind of the young craves knowledge but does not accept it. It is too proud to admit weakness and too timid to expose it.

When we are young, we look and see nothing. The real world is hidden from us behind clouds of fleeting perspectives. We are free to imagine, but we imagine with frivolity, without any sense of comprehension. By the time we begin to comprehend, youth has fled.

The land around the house, in which we stayed in Oregon, seemed incredibly beautiful. There were assorted trees and thick green foliage, horses roaming, dogs running and birds flying. I detached myself from the noise and began to write.

When darkness covered the land, everyone rushed to light the fireworks. The multicolored flames elevated high towards the sky and then vanished, like passing joys.

This beautiful family of good-hearted people that had embraced me were rejoicing and laughing and drinking and playing. Sometimes I wish I were like that, to rejoice at life's bright moments, even knowing that the fire surging to the sky would become a falling star within seconds.

For a few days, I was sick with the flu and spent much time in bed, with my pen in hand, writing. The third day my fever broke and, along with the temperature, the chain that was holding me in my remote cosmos seemed to break.

I was certain it was the peaceful land merging with the joy and the laughter of the people around me which forced me to observe the universe in its fullest dimension.

My companion wrapped her arms around me and I felt her tenderness.

Along with the fever, what was left of my youth's arrogance and inability to see and not seek, slowly left me. It was there where I truly felt a different kind of tenderness and love and that, coupled with my rebellious strength, began to heal my wounds and brought rhythm to my heart.

Nikos Ligidakis

Proud Dad on my sister's wedding day.

Mom and Dad with my brother Andreas on his wedding day.

36

READ, SHE SAID

It was one of those days that everything went wrong. The air conditioner broke down at the height of the desert summer heat. Some of the employees did not show up for work. I heard people complaining all day long about superficial problems. Then my sister called from the Greek Islands telling me it was beautiful there and that she wished I was with them. As I said, it was one of those days. My optimistic mind kept thinking that there is always tomorrow. I was glad the day at work was finally over. I walked to my car; there was a parking ticket under the windshield wiper. I threw it on the seat of the car thinking that this is nothing compared to the day I already had. On my way home, the right back tire went flat. I thought, okay, I can change it in a few minutes. Then I realized that I had no spare tire. Finally, after a considerable delay, I got home, anxious to put the day behind me. I poured a glass of water while I opened the mail - nothing but endless bills and charities asking for money. I threw it all on the table thinking; I'll deal with it tomorrow. Maybe a little television to be entertaining. Great, just in time for political bickering, murders, drug dealers, burning forests; nothing but distractions. Music has always been my escape, but on that day, I forced myself to go to sleep afraid to even listen to music. Lying in my bed, while I was in a time of half-asleep half-awake, reality began to warp. My consciousness dissolved into the gently lapping waves of dreaming, the world became a little more unreal, and my thoughts a bit more unbound. I've always loved that stage of the mind because it reveals unconventional views. While at that stage of consciousness, the night became morning. I stepped out the door to get the newspaper. The rays of the sun have taken away the moisture of the dawn; a sweet breeze touched my face and calmness overcame my mind. The beautiful blue sky inspired me to walk down the street. Strangely the road ahead was empty of people. I walked along until I reached a newspaper kiosk, like the one in my hometown, but in this one there were no candies and no newspapers. There were a few old dusty books forgotten on the counter. Further up by the town's square there were groups of people standing outside the coffeehouses. They spoke loudly, but I couldn't understand what they were saying. As I walked the street, while passing a building, I heard young children crying and, in another building, elders telling stories with painful voices. I quickened my steps to catch up with the sea of people walking on the streets of the agora, but I couldn't keep up with them. In the center of the city's square, under the statue of the fighters of freedom, a group of older ladies dressed in black stood before the statues; their faces were sober. One of them touched the stone of the statue softly. She ran her fingers through the names written on the marble, while at the end of the square children were running towards the ice cream truck.

The sunset guided me toward the outskirts of town, to a more peaceful environment; fishermen were returning from the deep sea and carpenters crafting wood. Soon I reached the grounds with the tall cypress trees. I sat under a tree to rest. The soft shadows of the cypress trees spread their soothing shadows on the timeworn headstones. Just a few meters beyond me there was the resting place of my mother and father. I talked to them for a while, asking questions and I assumed their answers. Before leaving, I placed on top of their grave my mother's favorite flowers; she loved lilies and orchids. Beyond the railroad tracks, there was an open field full of colorful flowers and further up, a dense forest. As my first steps entered that beautiful forest, I felt a mysterious feeling. I was overtaken with anxiety and sweat moistened my brow. Uncertain what I was afraid of, I stopped and looked around. The trees were at peace with nature; a soft breeze caressed their tops. A few harmless animals walked around untroubled by my presence. In the far horizon water streams twisting from the top of the high green mountains down to the lowlands. And beyond the treetops, there was the most beautiful sunset I had ever seen.

I thought, nothing to be afraid here – move on. I walked deeper into that forest with positive steps and a restless mind. Suddenly, I saw her. She was sitting under a blossomed almond tree, reading a book. A few other books were piled up next to the tree. As I approached her, she lifted her head to look at me. Her silky black long hair, the sweet smile warmed my heart and her deep brown eyes paralyzed my senses. She stretched her hands out to me. They looked like two branches with white flowers expanding from the almond tree. "I was expecting you," she said. I touched her hands and lifted her up. A long white dress was wrapped around her tall body. She looked directly into my eyes and my whole world came to a stop. I wanted to ask her name, but as I opened my mouth, she put her fingers over my lips. Right, I thought, how stupid of me! I already knew who she was. She was life, she was knowledge, she was wisdom. "This is yours to read," she said handing me a few books. I could not believe she was trusting me with that precious possession. I wanted to stay for a while to absorb the peacefulness, but she told me to go back to the world I came from. "Will you come with me?" I asked. "No, I must stay here." She said. "What if I have questions?" "Read," she said.

On my way back the world seemed different somehow. I stopped by the cemetery and brushed off the dry leaves from the top of my parents' grave. The old ladies, wearing spring dresses now, were sitting around the statue of the heroes, praying and the children kept running for ice cream. Down the street, I heard no children crying and there were people carrying gifts into the old people's home.

I leaned back in my chair outside the house by the forest. The years had gone by. My hair had turned white and my life was peaceful. My mind wandered into that path in the woods – it was so close. Through the large glass window, I glanced at the multiple shelves full of books inside the house. Every time I looked at them, I hear her voice - "Read," she said.

Nikos Ligidakis

My first school in Kiato

37

SOLILOGUE

I like to talk to myself; I've been doing it since I was a little boy. I blame the elders for this problem; those who gathered in the taverna to tell stories and talk about issues beyond the child's intellectual capacity. So, trying not to make a fool of myself, I listened to them and tried to analyze their words by talking to myself.

Oh, yeah, the elders told me that I was cute and adorable and gave me a few drachmas to go and get some ice cream - I did not want to be cute I wanted to be smart.

But what are you going to do? You are a child and there is no way to convince the adults that you are one of them – you don't look like one of them.

So, I listened, and I speculated and kept talking to myself.

This issue, what I thought to be a burden, has become a blessing. All the monologues of the past have piled up in my subconsciousness and periodically erupting in my brains, forcing me to write. One of the reasons I love writing is because, during the process of writing, I converse with myself. Some of these conversations are with my inner child and some with my alter ego. The subjects of this book are based on my first serious book. However back then, over twenty-five years ago, due to the language barriers, my thoughts did not translate precisely into the paper. The ideas were noble but by the time they became ink, were unclear and incomprehensible. After taking a lot of time to develop my writing skills and to expand my vocabulary of what used to be my third language, I believe the ink on paper now reflects my thoughts with a bit more clarity. It had taken a few years before my mind was able to rest from the emotional turbulence created by recycling sensitive subjects. However, the conflicts during my soliloquies have subsided and the intensity of my feelings have settled down.

The nighttime is when I make my confessions, when I confine myself to my torture chamber, my writing room, trying to unfold mysteries like my family's birthmark.

Over a century ago my father was born with a birthmark. The mark was a red round spot, high on the back of his neck. I don't know how far back into my father's family this birthmark appeared, but I do know that three of his five children carried this birthmark: my oldest brother, myself, and my sister. This birthmark keeps showing up on some members of the next generations as well. I understand that physically we resemble our ancestors, sometimes there is behavior resemblance, and we carry their genes, but this birthmark is a mystery to me.

And then there is Christmas. I am not sure if Christ was born on the day claiming to be his day of birth. Historians have different views on this subject. However, I know that I was born on that day because my mother told me so. I also know that my father left his last breath on Christmas morning, while he was abandoned to die on the cold sidewalk. Since the death of my father, Christmas has a bittersweet taste for me. It is the day I was born and the day my father died. Often, I wonder why my birth and his death happened on the same day and nearly at the same time, especially on a day of celebration. I have yet to master the subjects of fate, destiny and luck.

The notion that there is a natural order in the universe which cannot be changed, no matter how hard we try it is beyond my comprehension, so I keep talking to myself trying to understand what fate is.

Telling someone that he or she is destined for greatness since the day they are born is another enigmatic subject. It is difficult to believe that greatness could be achieved without having courage, altruism, temperance, and endurance.

And I had to convince myself that there is no such a thing as luck. When I played poker, trying to improve my poker skills, the element of luck was taken out of the equation. To consider that success is earned at a moment of magic, I was essentially telling myself that I could achieve success without trying harder. Another so-called mystery is my target skills. I had a slingshot when I was a child, but it was for a brief time because I was not good at aiming and killing birds. I remember how other young children took so much joy making their slingshots from the forks of tree branches. In the afternoons I would sneak out of the house and meet my friends at the nearby hill that was full of trees. That small woodland was full of birds, flying from tree to tree. Some of my friends were good at hitting birds and as they killed one of them, they will shout with enjoyment. I felt a knot in my stomach as I saw the birds falling from the trees – I did not understand the joy of killing. For the longest time, I tried to hit a bird, to be cool, to be a part of the gang, but could not do it. The stones out of my slingshot never could find their target. The other kids made fun of me, laughing at my incompetence.

Many years later when I was in the military, as I thought about my slingshot woes, I was determined to be on the best of the target shooting team. Surprisingly, the target marks were easy to hit. I was selected as one of the top-three target shooters in northern Greece. The mystery that haunted me growing up was solved. My inability to hit a live target was psychological; I did not want to take a life. And of course, I wanted to prove to my little friends that I wasn't incapable of hitting a target. It was over forty years ago the last time when I was in Kokinia, a suburb of Piraeus. It was there that I first played organized soccer on a soccer team playing in the lower divisions. I believe I was about thirteen years old. It is peculiar what yearnings about memories of the past surface from time to time.

It was mid-morning on a pleasant Saturday in September when I stepped off the bus to search for that old soccer field. As I walked the narrow streets, I realized that childhood memories were flying out from every direction. Although much has changed, the charm of the working-class neighborhoods remains intact. The scents and the scenery, reminiscent of the past, were alive. The small bakery from where the smell of fresh-baked bread is omnipresent; the furniture restorer, the shoemaker, the farmers market displaying rows of fruits and vegetables, the butcher shop, the fish market, the tables set outside the small restaurants; the outdoor movie theater where, later in the evening, people line up for tickets; the ice cream shop where mothers take their children for homemade ice cream. There is the kiosk in the corner of the small square which is boxed in by neoclassical buildings and outdoor cafes. And here it was; beyond the small square stood the soccer field, now larger and with stands. I remember the first day that I was given the team's jersey. "Did you bring your soccer shoes?" the coach asked me. I did not know what to say because I had no soccer shoes. Up to now none of the kids playing on the neighborhood grounds had any soccer shoes. He looked at me with pity and searched around to find an extra pair of shoes. "Here, he said, put them on." The problem was that those shoes were at least a size smaller but I wore them because I wanted to play. I remember my toes being squeezed and the hurt in my feet throughout the game. I never went back there again. Not sure what to call this experience that might have turned out differently if I had the right size shoes. I am sure it wasn't because of destiny or luck that I did not have soccer shoes.

I remembered when I tried to find my way in a strange country lost on unfamiliar streets at first. It was my choice to be there. My childhood yearnings watching the trains go by in my little town had become a reality, but it wasn't as I imagined it.

I hung the small bag with all my belongings over my shoulder and started walking towards an unknown direction, determined to find my way. I think I walked to the south, maybe north, or perhaps it could have been any other cardinal or intermediate direction.

As I moved on, I passed through different neighborhoods. Along the way, there was a street where people's home were the sidewalks and their beds were made of cardboard. Some of them stretched their hands to beg for help; genuinely heartbroken images.

Along the way, I saw ugly graffiti on the walls, drugs exchanging hands and there were sounds of gunfights.

At the end of those streets, there was a park with beautiful trees and thick green grass. Beyond the park, I observed mansions, high walls, secure gates and large, well-groomed yards.

As I was sitting between the two contrasting images; one of utmost despair the other in absolute comfort, I thought about fate and destiny. I believe it was there that I began to analyze the subjects. Growing up I did not witness prejudice or people sleeping on cardboard. I was surprised that on the roads I passed, there were no people on the sidewalks arguing about life, politics, or religion. On the contrary, people were in a hurry to get somewhere. They passed by as if they wanted to avoid contact with others. I could not understand why everyone was rushing along.

I kept on walking and crossed a long bridge. Underneath it were cars, thousands of them, moving slowly. I looked ahead to see where these cars were headed, but I couldn't see a clear destination. Nightfall began to darken the sky. I had to find a place to stay the night, for tomorrow was another day of searching for a clear direction.

"Hey man, can you spare some change?"

I saw an older man sitting on the street against the building. Next to him was a small pile of old clothes. I pulled some money from my pocket, and he thanked me. He was getting ready to spend the night on the cold sidewalk. For many people who walked by, he was nobody, just another homeless person without an identity.

"What is your name?" I asked him.

"My name is Abraham," he said. His voice seemed tired and his eyes sad.

I walked away, like everyone else, but at least now this man had an identity. His name was Abraham.

The destruction I saw on the streets blurred my vision temporary. The innocence of my childhood became distant memories among the social chaos. For a moment or two, I grew to be a misanthropist, thinking that rich people were snobs and the poor deserved to be treated with hostility. "It is their choice to be poor." I heard people saying. And for a moment or two, I began to believe it. My mind was infected with animosity; simple answers satisfied my ego, no time to think, I had work to do, I had to survive.

Suddenly, grandparents were not kind people, just old people in our way. Parents were not respectful images and children were not the source of joy. I've lost the ability to identify the good in people. Maybe it was the tortures of working hours or the resentment of feeling insignificant in this new and strange society; unable to comprehend the language and lifestyle.

I was young, eager to work, thirsty to learn. At a young age, I was studying to be an engineer now my hands were tirelessly washing dishes. I was a foosball wizard and a lot of money changed hands betting on my team's ability to win, now someone was throwing a dollar into my way of cleaning their table. I was about to be a soccer star, but now I was mopping floors. The wisdom of the elders in the taverna had become hordes of expressionless people who rushed in and out to eat and then lost into anonymity. My parents' expressions of love have become looks of contempt.

I was lost in the task of surviving myself, fighting social battles of my own; I did not have the time to see beyond my issues. I wanted people to know the pain in my face, to understand my struggles for survival; how selfish is that? All I saw was that most of them looked upon me as a dumb foreigner, one who couldn't speak and not able to navigate his way into the lifestyle of another culture. I choose to see arrogant people all around me. Thinking that they looked at me with contempt as if they were veritable saints and fonts of wisdom. Very few took the time to understand that they were shutting down my intellect. No one realized that I was a lover of culture. That I listened to Vivaldi and Tchaikovsky. That I read Plato, Kant, Tolstoy. That I admired Kennedy, King, Gandhi, and Mandela, that I too laughed at the comedy and cried at the tragedy. Eventually, I realized my selfishness. Was it me who looked at them with contempt because they spoke another language, they had different holidays and saluted a different flag? Was it me who refuse to reveal myself to strangers, kept that roar inside of me, determined to persist in the treacherous attitude that separated people?

It was a time that I refused to recount images that others had created. I could only be bonded with the reflection of my imagination, my own yearnings. To depend solely on people that felt closer to me.

Soon I began to find my way, to escape from exile, to steal from reality, to correct, to re-create, to see the characters that life had created. I began to search for people to talk to, to debate, to exchange ideas and feelings. Even though I knew deep in my heart that what separated people was the ideological pretense and that religious fanaticism turns people against people, I wanted to believe in humanity. What's the use? I thought at one time. The story will remain unchanged and unchangeable, yesterday, today, tomorrow, forever. It will always be the same, the story of man's mind, saying one thing and doing another. Even though that may be true, I replied that no, I was not like the others, that I was not about to treat others with contempt because they spoke another language, celebrated different holidays or believed in a different god. I promised to myself, to remember that – to remember that life lasts no longer than a desert flower; one that blossoms at daybreak and withers at sunset. See how life is, too, too short to waste it in anger and betrayal. Too short to shut down someone's humanity, someone's intellect. I decided to take a page of my shortcoming and learn a lesson from my treachery and foolishness.

The antagonists of all that makes us humans are arrogance and greed, two elements synonymous with supremacy, or to be exact, insecurity.

I thought of my journey and the roads I traveled to reach maturity.

My youth had been nothing but anxieties and questions as every route seemed to lead me to a dead end. It is true that when we are young, our thoughts revolve around two poles: apprehension and anticipation.

It is also true that in older age we stand fearlessly in front of uncertainty and tranquility.

This is a road that no one escapes, a formula of a life well-tested.

Even though waves of insanity roll over the human race, and military powers are hammering the militarily weak, I hold on to the breathtaking sunset, the scent of jasmine and caressing sea breeze, for dear life; to keep panic from overcoming me.

When finally, I felt a sense of relief, two words were refusing to go away. They were stuck in my psyche all the time and refused to leave me. The words were arrogance and greed, a catastrophic combination.

My Heroes, My Town

38

KIATO

There was another stop to make before coming back to America. My hometown of Kiato was a bit different than I remembered it, yet everything was so familiar. The impressive church of Agia Sotira loomed majestically in the middle of the town. The school from where the first rays of knowledge shone on the paths of my life was exactly as I had left it. The small port emerged from the blue sea to hold the fishing boats had not changed much. Taller buildings had sprung up along both sides of the streets and the agora was different now. Most of the people seemed unfamiliar. Some I recognized. A few elders stopped to tell me how my parents were revered in this town. My parents have long gone to their eternal sleep. They are resting in the town's cemetery, the beautiful place surrounded by cypress trees and located not too far from the sea.

In Kiato, I felt my mother's affectionate silence and my father's strict eyes. It is entirely impossible for me to escape the roots of my life's journey. It was there where I recognized joys and sorrows; it was there where I identified my responsibilities.

It was there that the ground and the sea spoke to me.

As I was about to end my trip to Greece, on these familiar grounds it seemed that the souls of my ancestors had risen, divulging the human struggles to me.

I knew, there and then, that it was only from history that we can identify our struggles.

To see the otherwise invisible enemy of peace; those who command people to kill and asked them to be killed. The real enemies are those who create conflicts, not those who engaged in it.

For me, it was in that little city that the first seeds of my duty were planted, and it was there that, I unconsciously understood that I must move my pen with clarity, to write whatever I felt in my heart. If it was about human suffering and soulful celebrations, let it be. If what I wrote wasn't intellectually brilliant or linguistically correct, then let it be.

My wish was to write my truth about emotional subjects - of this I was certain; of this, and nothing else.

Across from me, the old movie theater stood deserted, waiting to give its place to another structure, to create new memories, more convictions. Whatever structure takes its place, it will be difficult to recreate the memories that the old movie theater established during the past half of a century.

The movie theater was affectionately called, Cinema Paradiso, after the classic Italian movie. When I was a child, through its screen, my mind traveled to exotic places. It was on its screen that I observed the first kiss, seen the first battle, cheered for the good guys who chased bad guys and was introduced to the great intellectuals.

Sitting outside of the Cinema Paradiso, in the outdoor cafe, surrounded by the greenery of the city's square, I sipped my frappé.

The image of that little boy with the short pants and

the short haircut surfaced again in my mind. I glanced up at the sky. It was the same bright, blue sky I remembered from long ago. I felt the aura of the sea caressing my face and I felt the scent of freedom.

It was the feeling from my childhood when the days were simple and there were no worries between sunset and sunrise.

The sun was on its way west to set. It would have been around this hour that I would be heading to my father's taverna to ask him for money to go to the movies. Cinema Paradiso was new back then, new and very modern. During the summer months, the retractable roof would open and allow the viewers to watch the movies under the stars.

"J'accuse," I heard that voice again.

It was the voice of the nineteenth-century novelist, Emile Zola. His voice rang loud in my ears and brought my mind into a high stage of excitement.

Emile Zola devoted his life to exposing corruption just before World War One in France. His famous letter "J'accuse" served to bring attention to the Dreyfus case.

Dreyfus was sent to Devils Island when he was convicted of espionage. It was Zola who accused the powerful French military of complicity and cover-up.

Because of that, Dreyfus was eventually cleared and restored to military ranks.

It was back then, watching Zola's life story, that for the first time, I felt the powerful effect of writing. It was back then that I noticed the inerasable message written in ink and how the pen that is pressed powerfully against the paper leaves behind timeless phrases.

What an extraordinary gift fantasy is!

With fantasy, you can go where you like, and you can be what you want.

With fantasy, you can invert reality, and you can foresee things that others cannot see.

I left my Cinema Paradiso behind, holding the memories dear in my heart.

I walked towards the cemetery. An urge to talk to my parents overcame me.

I wanted to tell them thank you for the life they gave me, for the extraordinary conviction that, silently, affectionately and strictly had inflamed my heart.

It was because of them that I have learned to honor human life, to controvert conflicts, and to oppose egocentric beliefs aimed to oppress and destroy.

This is the gift that they left behind for me. This and not much more!

Their gravesides were well manicured. My siblings had taken out the old marble stone that covered their grave and replaced it with a new one. Pure white pieces of marble were arranged around the large marble stone. I placed fresh flowers next to their candle, a candle that was burning an eternal flame of humanity and gallantry.

I spoke to them for a while. When I left them behind, the well-manicured graveside reminded me of my father's fresh shaved face, wearing his white shirt, and of my mother's just washed hair and her favorite flowered spring dress.

I walked back to the streets of Kiato. The elders, sitting in the coffee shops, took time to tell me more stories of long ago.

I walked by the seaport and felt an inexplicable joy. I looked at the sea, its waves lifting gently, gleaming under the sunlight.

I felt my heart following their rhythm and I became the sea. I was reminded of my endless voyages full of adventures. After a global journey, I have arrived here, where it all began – my beloved blue waters of Greece. It is from those waters that I had initially boarded a ship and departed. Where to? Who knew?

It was the winds of life that blew on my back and showed me the routes.

It was in this little town that my forefathers taught me one of the most important conviction: Don't be afraid to love the world.

The time came for me to go, to head back to America, where my children and grandchildren awaited me.

My mother's silent tenderness and my father's strict eyes followed me there, again, as they will till the end of time.

My Heroes, My Town

About the Author

Award winning author, Nikos Ligidakis, writes with clarity and passion in an ardent voice, not to just recount adventures, but with an expression of feelings, to encourage the reader to think, to find hope in the eternal struggle for the meaning of life and the awareness of harmony.

Today Nikos devotes his life to coaching new authors encouraging and assisting them to write and publish their books.

Nikos has founded several charitable organizations with the most notable his Thanksgiving Project to Feed the Hungry, a program that provided food to tens of thousands during its 21-year run. His selfless work with people has earned him several humanitarian awards over the years.

"As a writer, my aspiration has always been to share my perspective on what it means to be a human being, in all its complexities. I wanted to tell a story that reflects a comparative importance of political structures, religions and histories of the past. My books represent a lifelong dream of putting into narrative form, my many observations of the brilliance and kindness of the human spirit: people at their worst and people at their best. It is my intention to engage the reader in the process of observing history in both times past and in current day happenings for the sole purpose of gaining greater clarity in the shaping of one's own approach to life and the deepening of individual insight."

Nikos Ligidakis